How to Make a Massachusetts Will

HOW TO
MAKE A
MASSACHUSETTS
WILL

with forms

Joseph P. DiBlasi
Mark Warda
Attorneys at Law

Sphinx® Publishing
A Division of Sourcebooks, Inc.
Naperville, IL • Clearwater, FL

Second edition, 1999

Published by: **Sourcebooks, Inc.®**

Naperville Office
P.O. Box 372
Naperville, Illinois 60566
630-961-3900
Fax: 630-961-2168

Clearwater Office
P.O. Box 25
Clearwater, Florida 33757
727-587-0999
Fax: 727-586-5088

Interior Design and Production: Amy S. Hall, Sourcebooks, Inc.®

This publication is designed to provide accurate and authoritative information in regard to the subject matter covered. It is sold with the understanding that the publisher is not engaged in rendering legal, accounting, or other professional service. If legal advice or other expert assistance is required, the services of a competent professional person should be sought.

From a Declaration of Principles Jointly Adopted by a Committee of the
American Bar Association and a Committee of Publishers and Associations

Library of Congress Cataloging-in-Publication Data
DiBlasi, Joseph P.
    How to make a Massachusetts will : with forms / Joseph P.
DiBlasi, Mark Warda. -- 2nd ed.
        p.   cm.
    Includes index.
    ISBN 1-57248-108-0 (pbk.)
    1. Wills--Massachusetts Popular works. 2. Wills--Massachusetts
Forms.   I. Warda, Mark. II. Title.
KFM2544.Z9D53   1999
346.74405'4--dc21
                                                    99-31258
                                                        CIP

Printed and bound in the United States of America.

Paperback — 10 9 8 7 6 5 4 3 2

CONTENTS

Using Self-Help Law Books

Whenever you shop for a product or service, you are faced with various levels of quality and price. In deciding what product or service to buy, you make a cost/value analysis on the basis of your willingness to pay and the quality you desire.

When buying a car, you decide whether you want transportation, comfort, status, or sex appeal. Accordingly, you decide among such choices as a Neon, a Lincoln, a Rolls Royce, or a Porsche. Before making a decision, you usually weigh the merits of each option against the cost.

When you get a headache, you can take a pain reliever (such as aspirin) or visit a medical specialist for a neurological examination. Given this choice, most people, of course, take a pain reliever, since it costs only pennies; whereas a medical examination costs hundreds of dollars and takes a lot of time. This is often the most logical choice: it's rare to need anything more than a pain reliever for a headache. But in some cases, a headache may indicate a brain tumor, and failing to see a specialist right away can result in complications. Should everyone with a headache go to a specialist? Of course not, but people treating their own illnesses must realize that they are betting on the basis of their cost/value analysis of the situation; they are taking the most logical option.

The same cost/value analysis must be made in deciding to do one's own legal work. Many legal situations are very straight forward, requiring a simple form and no complicated analysis. Anyone with a little intelligence and a book of instructions can handle the matter without outside help.

But there is always the chance that complications are involved that only an attorney would notice. To simplify the law into a book like this, several legal cases often must be condensed into a single sentence or paragraph. Otherwise, the book would be several hundred pages long and too complicated for most people. However, this simplification necessarily leaves out many details and nuances that would apply to special or unusual situations. Also, there are many ways to interpret most legal questions. Your case may come before a judge who disagrees with the analysis of our authors.

Therefore, in deciding to use a self-help law book and to do your own legal work, you must realize that you are making a cost/value analysis. You have decided that the money you will save in doing it yourself outweighs the chance your case will not turn out to your satisfaction. Most people handling their own simple legal matters never have a problem, but occasionally people find that it ended up costing them more to have an attorney straighten out the situation than it would have if they had hired an attorney in the beginning. Keep this in mind while handling your case, and be sure to consult an attorney if you feel you might need further guidance.

Introduction

This book was written to help Massachusetts' residents make their own wills quickly and easily without the expense or delay of hiring a lawyer. It begins with a short explanation of how a will works and what a will can and cannot do. It is designed to allow those with simple estates to quickly and inexpensively set up their affairs to distribute their property according to their wishes. It includes an explanation of how such things as joint property and *pay on death* accounts will affect your planning.

It also includes information on appointing a guardian for any minor children you may have. This can be useful in avoiding bad feelings between relatives and in protecting the children from being raised by someone to whom you would object.

Chapters 1 through 7 explain the laws that affect the making of a will. Appendix A contains sample filled-in will forms to show you how it is done. Appendix B contains blank will forms you can use. A flow chart in appendix C will help you choose the right will form based upon your circumstances and desires. There is also a glossary with a list of terms.

You can prepare your own will quickly and easily by using the forms out of the book, or by photocopying them, or you can retype the material on sheets of paper. The small amount of time it takes to do this can give you and your loved ones the peace of mind of knowing that your estate will be distributed according to your wishes.

A surprising number of people have had their estates pass to the wrong parties because of a simple lack of knowledge of how the laws work. Before using any of the forms in appendix B, you should read and understand all of the chapters in this book.

In each example given in the text, you might ask, "What if the spouse died first?" or "What if the children were grown up?" and the answer might be different. If your situation is at all complicated, you are advised to seek the advice of an attorney. In many communities, wills are available for very reasonable prices. No book of this type can cover every contingency in every case, but a knowledge of the basics will help you to make the right decisions regarding your property.

The forms in this book are for simple wills to leave property to your family, or if you have no family, to friends or charities. As explained in chapter 3, if you wish to disinherit your family and leave your property to others, you should consult with an attorney who can be sure that your will cannot be successfully challenged in court.

There is no worse torture than the torture of laws.

—Francis Bacon

BASIC RULES YOU SHOULD KNOW

1

Before making your will, you should understand how a will works and what it can and cannot do. Otherwise, your plans may not be carried out and the wrong people may end up with your property.

WHAT IS A WILL?

A will is a document you can use to control who gets your property, who will be guardian of your children and their property, and who will manage your estate upon your death.

HOW A WILL IS USED

Some people think a will avoids probate; it does not. A will is the document used in probate to determine who receives the property, and who is appointed guardian and executor.

AVOIDING PROBATE

If you wish to avoid probate, you need to use methods other than a will, such as joint ownership, pay-on-death accounts, or living trusts. The first two of these are discussed later in this chapter. For information on living trusts, you should refer to a book which focuses on trusts as used for estate planning. *Living Trusts and Simple Ways to Avoid Probate* is available from the publisher of this book.

If a person successfully avoids probate with all of his or her property, he or she may not need a will. In most cases, when a husband or wife dies no will or probate is necessary because everything is owned jointly. However, everyone should have a will in case some property, that one forgot to put into joint ownership or that was received just prior to death, does not avoid probate for some reason, or if both husband and wife die in the same accident.

JOINT TENANCY AVOIDS PROBATE

Property that is owned in *joint tenancy with right of survivorship* does not pass under a will. If a will gives property to one person but it is already in a joint account with another person, the will is usually ignored and the joint owner of the account gets the property. This is because the property in the account avoids probate and passes directly to the joint owner. A will only controls property that goes through probate. There are exceptions to this rule. If money is put into a joint account only for convenience, it might pass under the will; but if the joint owner does not give it up, it could take an expensive court battle to get it back.

Putting property into joint tenancy does not give absolute rights to it. If the estate owes estate taxes, the recipient of joint tenancy property may have to contribute to the tax payment. Also, some states give spouses a right to property that is in joint accounts with other people. This is explained later in this chapter.

EXAMPLES
☛ Ted and his wife want all of their property to go to the survivor of them. They put their house, cars, bank accounts, and brokerage accounts in joint ownership. When Ted dies, his wife only has to show his death certificate to get all the property transferred to her name. No probate or will is necessary.

☞ After Ted's death, his wife, Michelle, puts all of the property and accounts into joint ownership with her son, Mark. Upon Michelle's death, Mark needs only to present her death certificate to have everything transferred into his name. No probate or will is necessary.

JOINT TENANCY OVERRULES YOUR WILL

If all property is in joint ownership or if all property is distributed through a will, things are simple. But when some property passes by each method, a person's plans may not be fulfilled.

EXAMPLES

☞ Bill's will leaves all his property to his sister, Mary. Bill dies owning a house jointly with his wife, Joan, and a bank account jointly with his son, Don. Upon Bill's death Joan gets the house, Don gets the bank account and his sister, Mary, gets nothing.

☞ Betty's will leaves half her assets to Ann and half her assets to George. Betty dies owning $1,000,000 in stock jointly with George, and a car in her name alone. Ann gets only a half interest in the car. George gets all the stock and a half interest in the car.

☞ John's will leaves all his property equally to his five children. Before going in the hospital he puts his oldest son, Harry, as a joint owner of his accounts. John dies and Harry gets all of his assets. The rest of the children get nothing.

In each of these cases, the property went to a person it probably shouldn't have because the decedent didn't realize that joint ownership overruled his or her will. In some families, this might not be a problem. Harry might divide the property equally (and possibly pay a gift tax). But in many cases Harry would just keep everything and the family would never talk to him again, or would take him to court.

Joint Tenancy Can Be Risky

In many cases, joint property can be an ideal way to own property and avoid probate. However it does have risks. If you put your real estate in joint ownership with someone, you cannot sell it or mortgage it without that person's signature. If you put your bank account in joint ownership with someone they can take out all of your money.

EXAMPLES

☛ Alice put her house in joint ownership with her son. She later married Ed and moved in with him. She wanted to sell her house and to invest the money for income. Her son refused to sign the deed because he wanted to keep the home in the family. She was in court for ten months getting her house back and the judge almost refused to do it.

☛ Alex put his bank accounts into joint ownership with his daughter Mary to avoid probate. Mary fell in love with Doug who was in trouble with the law. Doug talked Mary into "borrowing" $30,000 from the account for a "business deal" that went sour. Later she "borrowed" $25,000 more to pay Doug's bail bond. Alex didn't find out until it was too late that his money was gone.

"Tenancy in Common" Does Not Avoid Probate

In Massachusetts as in most states, there are three basic ways to own property, joint tenancy with right of survivorship, tenancy in common, and an estate by the entireties. *Joint tenancy with right of survivorship* means that if one owner of the property dies, the survivor automatically gets the decedent's share. *Tenancy in common* means when one owner dies, that owner's share of the property goes to his or her heirs or beneficiaries under the will. *An estate by the entireties* is like joint tenancy with right of survivorship, but it can only apply to a married couple and is only recognized in some states.

EXAMPLES

☞ Tom and Marcia bought a house together and lived together for twenty years but were never married. The deed did not specify joint tenancy. When Tom died, his bother inherited his half of the house and it had to be sold because Marcia could not afford to buy it from him.

☞ Lindsay and her husband Rocky bought a house. When Rocky suddenly died, Lindsay obtained full ownership of the house by filing a death certificate at the Registry of Deeds. That was because the deed to the house stated that they were husband and wife so ownership was presumed to be tenancy by the entireties.

A Spouse Can Overrule a Will

Under Massachusetts law, a surviving spouse, upon waiver of the will, is entitled to a minimum share of the decedent's estate no matter what the will says. This is sometimes called the *forced share* or *elective share*. The amount of the forced share varies depending on whether the decedent also leaves issue and/or kin.

If Issue Survive

If issue (i.e., children, grandchildren, or great-grandchildren) survive, the surviving spouse is entitled to one-third of the personal property and one-third of the real property (house) in the estate. If, however, the forced share would exceed $25,000, the spouse is entitled to real or personal property worth $25,000 and a life interest in the amount by which that one-third share exceeds the $25,000.

If Only Kin Survive

If the decedent only leaves kin and no issue, the surviving spouse, upon waiver of the will, is entitled to $25,000 outright and life interest in one-half of the remaining personal property and one-half the remaining real property.

If No Issue or Kin Survive

If the decedent does not leave issue or kin, then the surviving spouse, upon waiver of the will, is entitled to $25,000 plus one-half of the remaining personal property and real property outright.

EXAMPLES
- ☞ John's will leaves all of his property (worth $18,000) to his children of a prior marriage and nothing to his second wife who is already wealthy. Since issue survive, the wife, by waiving the will, gets one-third, or $6,000.

- ☞ Mary, who is married but without children, puts half of her property in a joint account with her husband and in her will she leaves all of her other property to her sister. When she dies, her husband gets all the money in the joint account and $25,000 outright with a life-interest in one-half of both the remaining real and personal property.

A SPOUSE'S SHARE CAN BE AVOIDED

While some feel it is wrong to avoid giving a spouse the share allowed by law, there are legitimate reasons for doing so (such as where there are children from a prior marriage) and the law allows exceptions.

The easiest way is for your spouse to sign a written agreement either before or after the marriage. While many spouses express the greatest fondness for their stepchildren, getting them to sign over a large share of an estate can be a challenge. When such an agreement is signed before marriage, it is called a *premarital agreement* or *antenuptial agreement;* and when it is signed during the marriage, it is called a *marital agreement.* Check with the publisher of this book for a book on premarital agreements.

Another way to avoid a spouse's share is by owning property in joint tenancy or in a trust. Such property avoids probate and the spouse cannot make a claim to it.

EXAMPLE
- ☞ Dan owns his stocks jointly with his son. He owns his bank accounts jointly with his daughter. If he has no other property, his spouse gets nothing since there is no property in his estate.

In recent years, Massachusetts probate lawyers have been trying to change the law so that a spouse receives a share or all property that passes at death, not just property in probate. Another proposal is to give a spouse a percentage of all property but to make the size of it dependent upon the length of the marriage. For example, after a one-year marriage the spouse would get three percent but after a fifteen year marriage the spouse would receive fifty percent. None of these proposals have passed the legislature at the time of publication of this book, but you should be aware that the law may change in the future.

If the law changes to include all property at death, the best ways to avoid the spouse's share would be an agreement with your spouse as explained above, life insurance naming other parties as beneficiaries, or gifts to them during your life.

Avoiding a spouse's share, especially without his or her knowledge, opens the possibility of a lawsuit after your death, and if your actions were not done to precise legal requirements, they could be dismissed. Therefore, you should consider consulting an attorney if you plan to leave your spouse less than the share provided by law.

I/T/F Bank Accounts Are Better than Joint Ownership

One way of keeping bank accounts out of your estate and still retain control is to title them *in trust for* or I/T/F with a named a beneficiary. Some banks may use the letters POD for *pay on death* or TOD for *transfer on death*. Either way the result is the same. No one except you can get the money until your death, and on death it immediately goes directly to the person you name, without a will or probate proceeding. These are sometimes called *Totten Trusts* after the court case that declared them legal.

EXAMPLE   ☛ Rich opened a bank account in the name of "Rich, I/T/F Mary." If Rich dies, the money automatically goes to Mary. Prior to his death,

Mary has no control over the account, doesn't even have to know about it, and Rich can take Mary's name off the account at any time.

Now Securities Can Be Registered I/T/F

The drawback of the Totten Trust has been that it was only good for cash in a bank account. Stocks and bonds still had to go through probate. But a new law has been passed by over half the states which allows people to register their stock, bonds, mutual funds and other securities in the I/T/F form.

Unfortunately, Massachusetts has not yet passed this law, but you may be able to take advantage of it. If your mutual fund or brokerage account is with a company in one of the states which allows such registration, you can set up an I/T/F account. Check with your broker or mutual fund. If they cannot offer I/T/F accounts, it might be worth changing to one who does.

You need to have your securities correctly registered in order to set them up to transfer automatically. If you use a brokerage account, the brokerage company should have a form for you to do this.

Getting Married Automatically Changes Your Will

If you get married after making your will and do not rewrite it after the wedding, your spouse gets a share of your estate as if you had no will unless you have a pre-nuptial agreement, or if you made a provision for your spouse in the will.

EXAMPLE
☞ John made out his will leaving everything to his physically-challenged brother. When he married Joan, an heiress with plenty of money, he didn't change his will because he still wanted his brother to get his estate. When he died, Joan received John's entire estate, and John's brother got nothing.

GETTING DIVORCED AUTOMATICALLY CHANGES YOUR WILL

A judgment of divorce automatically changes your will to the effect that the former spouse is treated as if he or she predeceased the maker of the will.

HAVING CHILDREN AUTOMATICALLY CHANGE YOUR WILL

If you have a child after making your will and do not rewrite it, the child may receive a share of your estate as if there was no will.

EXAMPLE

☛ Dave made a will leaving half his estate to his sister and the other half to be shared by his three children. He later has another child and doesn't revise his will. Upon his death his fourth child would get one quarter of his estate, his sister would get three-eighths and the other three children would each get one-eighth.

It is best to rewrite your will at the birth of a child. However, another solution is to include the following clause after the names of your children in your will.

```
"...and any afterborn children living at the
time of my death, in equal shares."
```

If you have one or more children and are leaving all of your property to your spouse, your will would not be affected by the birth of a subsequent child.

How Your Debts Are Paid

One of the duties of the person administering an estate is to pay the debts of the decedent. Before an estate is distributed, the legitimate debts must be ascertained and paid.

An exception is *secured debts*, these are debts that are protected by a lien against property, like a home loan or a car loan. In the case of a secured debt, the loan does not have to be paid before the property is distributed.

EXAMPLE
☞ John owns a $100,000 house with a $80,000 mortgage and he has $100,000 in the bank. If he leaves the house to his brother and the bank account to his sister, then his brother would receive the home but would owe the $80,000 mortgage.

What if your debts are more than your property? Today, unlike hundreds of years ago, people cannot inherit other peoples' debts. A person's property is used to pay their probate administration expenses first, followed by their last illness and funeral expenses. After these debts are paid, if there is not enough left from the estate to pay all of the decedent's debts, the remaining debts will be paid according to the type (or class) of debt. If there are insufficient assets to pay all of the debts from the next particular class, creditors of that class will be paid on a pro-rata basis. Creditors of all lower classes will be out of luck. However, if a person leaves property to people and does not have enough assets to pay his or her debts, the property will be sold to pay the debts.

EXAMPLE
☞ Jeb's will leaves all of his property to his three children. At the time of his death, Jeb, has $30,000 in medical bills, $11,000 in credit card debt, and his only assets are his car and $5,000 in stock. The car and stock would be sold and the funeral bill and probate fees paid out of the proceeds. If any money was left it would go to the creditors and nothing would be left for the children. The children would not have to pay the medical bills or credit card debt.

ESTATE AND INHERITANCE TAXES

For Massachusetts residents dying on or after January 1, 1997, there no longer is an independent Massachusetts estate tax. Instead, a sponge tax will replace the estate tax. With the sponge tax, no additional tax is due to Massachusetts, however, Massachusetts receives (or sponges) revenue as a result of a credit given for the federal estate tax due.

There is a federal estate tax for estates above a certain amount. Estates below that amount are allowed a *unified credit* which exempts them from tax. The unified credit applies to the estate a person can leave at death and to gifts during his or her lifetime. In 1999, the amount exempted by the unified credit is $650,000 but it will rise to $1,000,000 by the year 2006. The amount will change according to the following schedule.

Year	Amount
1999	$650,000
2000-2001	$675,000
2002-2003	$700,000
2004	$850,000
2005	$950,000
2006	$1,000,000

ANNUAL EXCLUSION

When a person makes a gift, that gift is subtracted from the amount entitled to the unified credit available to his or her estate at death. However, a person is allowed to make gifts of up to $10,000 per person per year without having these subtracted from the unified credit. This means a married couple can make gifts of up to $20,000 per person. The Taxpayer Relief Act of 1997 provided that this exclusion amount will be adjusted for inflation.

There are two things in which men, in other things wise enough, do usually miscarry; in putting off the making of their wills and their repentance until it is too late.
—Tillotson

DO YOU NEED A MASSACHUSETTS WILL?

2

WHAT A WILL CAN DO

BENEFICIARIES

A will allows you to decide who gets your property after your death. You can give specific personal items to certain persons and choose which of your friends or relatives, if any, deserve a greater share of your estate. You can also leave gifts to schools and charities.

EXECUTOR

A will allows you to decide who will be in charge of handling your estate. This is the person who gathers together all your assets and distributes them to the beneficiaries, hires attorneys or accountants if necessary, and files any essential tax or probate forms. In Massachusetts, this person is called the *executor* (*executrix* if female). (In other states, he or she is called the *personal representative*.) With a will, you can provide that your personal representative does not have to post a surety bond with the court in order to serve and this can save your estate some money. You can also give him or her the power to sell your property and take other actions without getting a court order.

GUARDIAN

A will allows you to choose a guardian for your minor children. This way you can avoid fights among relatives and make sure the best person raises your children. You may also appoint separate guardians over your children and over their money. For example you may appoint your sister as guardian over your children, and your father as guardian over their money. That way, a second person can keep an eye on how the children's money is being spent.

PROTECTING
HEIRS

You can set up a trust to provide that your property is not distributed immediately. Many people feel that their children would not be ready to handle large sums of money at the age of majority, which in most states is eighteen. A will can direct that the money is held until the children are twenty-one, or twenty-five, or older.

MINIMIZING
TAXES

If your estate is over the amount protected by the federal *unified credit* ($650,000 in 1999 but will be rising to $1,000,000 by the year 2006), it will be subject to federal estate taxes. If you wish to lower those taxes, for example by making gifts to charities, you can do so through a will. However, such estate planning is beyond the scope of this book and you should consult an estate planning attorney or another book for further information.

WHAT IF YOU HAVE NO WILL?

If you do not have a will, Massachusetts law provides that your property shall be distributed as follows:

- ☞ If you leave a spouse and no children or issue, your spouse gets your entire estate if the whole estate does not exceed $200,000 in value. If it is greater than $200,000, the spouse takes $200,000 plus half of the remainder of the estate.

- ☞ If you leave a spouse and at least one child (or issue), your spouse gets half of your estate and your children get equal shares of the other half.

- ☞ If you leave no spouse, all of your children get equal shares of your estate. If one of your children predeceases you but leaves children of his own, those children will share equally in their parent's share.

☛ If you leave no spouse and no children, your estate would go to the highest persons on the following list who are living.

 • your parents

 • your brothers and sisters, or if dead, their children

 • next of kin in equal degree (If there are two or more collateral kindred in equal degree claiming through different ancestors, those claiming through the nearest ancestor shall be preferred.)

☛ If you die without a will and leave no spouse and no kindred, your property is transferred (*escheats*) to the Commonwealth of Massachusetts.

IS YOUR OUT-OF-STATE WILL VALID IN MASSACHUSETTS?

A will that is valid in another state would probably be valid to pass property in Massachusetts. However, if the will is not "self-proved," before it could be accepted by a Massachusetts Probate Court, a person in your former state would have to be appointed as a "Commissioner" to take the oath of a person who witnessed your signature on the will. Because of the expense and delay in having a Commissioner appointed and the problems in finding out-of-state witnesses, it is advisable to execute a new will after moving to Massachusetts.

Another advantage to having a Massachusetts will is that as a Massachusetts resident your estate will pay no state probate or inheritance taxes. If you move to Massachusetts but keep your old will, your former state of residence may try to collect taxes on your estate.

Massachusetts also allows a will to be *self-proved* so that the witnesses never have to be called in to take an oath. With special self-proving language in your will, the witnesses take the oath at the time of signing and never have to be seen again.

EXAMPLE
☛ George and Barbara left their high-tax state and retired to Massachusetts, which has no estate or inheritance taxes, but they never made a new will. Upon their deaths, their former state of residence tried to collect a tax from their estate because their old wills stated that they were residents of that state.

WHO CAN MAKE A MASSACHUSETTS WILL?

Any person who is eighteen years of age and of sound mind can make a valid will in Massachusetts.

WHAT A WILL CANNOT DO

A will cannot direct that anything illegal be done and it cannot put unreasonable conditions on a gift. A provision that your daughter gets all of your property if she divorces her husband would be ignored by the court. She would get the property with no conditions attached. You can put some conditions in your will. You should consult with an attorney to be sure they are enforceable.

A will cannot leave money or property to an animal because animals cannot legally own property. If you wish to continue paying for care of an animal after your death, you should leave the funds in trust or to a friend whom you know will care for the animal.

WHO CAN USE A SIMPLE WILL?

The wills in this book will pass your property whether your estate is $1,000 or $100,000,000. However, if your estate is over $650,000 (this amount will rise to $1,000,000 by the year 2006) then you might be able to avoid estate taxes by using a trust or other tax-saving device. The larger your estate, the more you can save on estate taxes by doing more complicated planning. If you have a large estate and are concerned about estate taxes, you should consult an estate planning attorney or a book on estate planning.

WHO SHOULD NOT USE A SIMPLE WILL?

WILL CONTEST

If you expect that there may be a fight over your estate or that someone might contest your will's validity, you should consult a lawyer. If you leave less than the statutory share of your estate to your spouse or if you leave one or more of your children out of your will, it is likely that someone will contest your will.

COMPLICATED ESTATES

If you are the beneficiary of a trust or have any complications in your legal relationships, you may need special provisions in your will.

BLIND OR UNABLE TO WRITE

A person who is blind or who can sign only with an "X" should also consult a lawyer about the proper way to make and execute a will.

ESTATES OVER $650,000

If you expect to have over $650,000 (this amount will rise to $1,000,000 by the year 2006) at the time of your death, you may want to consult with a CPA or tax attorney regarding tax consequences.

CONDITIONS

If you wish to put some sort of conditions or restrictions on the property you leave, you should consult a lawyer. For example, if you want to leave money to your brother only if he quits smoking, or to a hospital only if they name a wing in your honor, you should consult an attorney to be sure that your conditions are valid.

What you leave at your death let it be without controversy, else the lawyers will be your heirs.
—F. Osborn

HOW TO MAKE A SIMPLE WILL 3

IDENTIFYING PARTIES IN YOUR WILL

PEOPLE

When making your will, it is important to clearly identify the persons you name as your beneficiaries. In some families, names differ only by middle initial or by Jr. or Sr. Be sure to check everyone's name before making your will. You can also add your relationship to the beneficiary, and their location such as "my cousin, Laura Genca, now or formerly of Woburn, Massachusetts."

ORGANIZATIONS

The same applies to organizations and charities. For example, there is more than one group using the words "cancer society" or "heart association" in their name. Be sure to get the correct name of the group to that you intend to leave your gift.

SPOUSE AND CHILDREN

It is a good idea to mention your spouse and children in your will even if you do not leave them any property. That is to show that you are of sound mind and know who are your heirs. As mentioned earlier, if you have a spouse and/or children and plan to leave your property to persons other than them, you should consult an attorney to be sure that your will will be enforceable.

Personal Property

Because people acquire and dispose of personal property so often, it is not advisable to list a lot of small items in your will. Otherwise, when you sell or replace one of them you may have to rewrite your will.

One solution is to describe the type of item you wish to give. For example, instead of saying, "I leave my 1998 Ford to my sister," you should say, "I leave any automobile I own at the time of my death to my sister."

Of course, if you do mean to give a specific item, you should describe it. For example instead of "I leave my diamond ring to Joan," you should say, "I leave to Joan the one-half carat diamond ring which I inherited from my grandmother," because you might own more than one diamond ring at the time of your death. (Hopefully!)

HANDWRITTEN LIST OF PERSONAL PROPERTY

In Massachusetts, you are allowed to leave a handwritten list of personal items (other than money or property used in a trade or business) that you wish to go to certain people and this would be legally binding. The wills in this book include a clause stating that you may leave such a list. This list must be signed by you. It may be made before or after your will and it may be changed at any time. It does not need to be witnessed.

Specific Bequests

Occasionally, a person will want to leave a little something to a friend or charity and the rest to the family. This can be done with a *specific bequest* such as "$1,000 to my dear friend, Martha Jones." Of course, there could be a problem if, at the time of a person's death, there wasn't anything left after the specific bequests.

EXAMPLE

☛ At the time of making his will, Todd had $1,000,000 in assets. He felt generous so he left $50,000 to a local hospital, $50,000 to a local group that took care of homeless animals and the rest to his children. Unfortunately, several years later, the stock market crashed and he committed suicide by jumping off a bridge. His estate at the time was worth only $110,000 so after the above specific bequests and the legal fees and expenses of probate, there was nothing left for his five children.

Another problem with specific bequests is that some of the property may be worth considerably more or less at death than when the will was made.

EXAMPLE ☞ Joe wanted his two children to equally share his estate. His will left his son his stocks (worth $500,000 at the time) and his daughter $500,000 in cash. By the time of Joe's death the stock was only worth $100,000.

He should have left "fifty percent" of his estate to each child. If giving certain things to certain people is an important part of your estate plan, you can give specific items to specific persons, but remember to make changes if your assets change.

JOINT BENEFICIARIES Be careful about leaving one item of personal property to more than one person. For example, if you leave something to your son and his wife, what would happen if they divorce? Even if you leave something to two of your own children, what if they can't agree about who will have possession of it? Whenever possible, leave property to one person.

RESIDUE CLAUSE

One of the most important clauses in a will is the *residue clause*. This is the clause that says something like "all the rest of my property I leave to…" This clause makes sure that the will disposes of all property owned at the time of death and that nothing is forgotten.

The best way to distribute property in a simple will is to put it all in the residue clause. In the first example in the previous section, the problem would have been avoided if the will had read as follows: "The rest, residue, and remainder of my estate I leave, five percent to ABC

Hospital, five percent to XYZ Animal Welfare League and ninety percent to be divided equally among my children..."

ALTERNATE BENEFICIARIES

You should always provide for an *alternate beneficiary* in case the person you name dies before you and you do not have a chance to make out a new will.

SURVIVOR OR
DESCENDANTS

Suppose your will leaves your property to your sister and brother but your brother predeceases you. Should his share go to your sister or to your brother's children or grandchildren?

If you are giving property to two or more persons and if you want it all to go to the other if one of them dies, then you would specify "or the survivor of them."

If, on the other hand, you want the property to go to the children of the deceased person you should state in your will, "or their lineal descendants." This would include his or her children and grandchildren.

FAMILY OR
PERSON

If you decide you want it to go to your brother's children and grandchildren, you must next decide if an equal share should go to each family or to each person. For example, if your brother leaves three grandchildren, and one is an only child of his daughter and the others are the children of his son, should all grandchildren get equal shares, or should they take their parent's share?

When you want each family to get an equal share it is called *per stirpes*. When you want each person to get an equal share it is called *per capita*. Most of the wills in this book use per stirpes because that is the most common way property is left. If you wish to leave your property per capita, you can rewrite the will with this change.

EXAMPLE

☛ Alice leaves her property to her two daughters, Mary and Pat in equal shares, or to their lineal descendants per stirpes. Both daughters die before Alice. Mary leaves one child; Pat leaves two children. In this case, Mary's child would get half of the estate and Pat's children would split the other half of the estate. If Alice had specified per capita instead of per stirpes then each child would have gotten one-third of the estate.

Per Stirpes Distribution

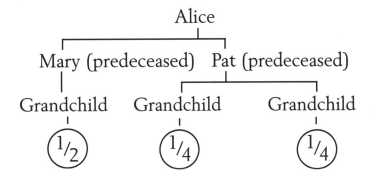

Per Capita Distribution

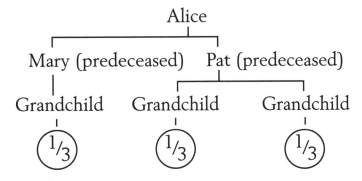

There are fourteen different will forms in this book that should cover the options most people want, but you may want to divide your property slightly differently from what is stated in these forms. If so, you can retype the forms according to these rules, specifying whether the property should go to the survivor or the lineal descendants. If this is confusing to you, you should consider seeking the advice of an attorney.

SURVIVORSHIP

Many people put a clause in their will stating that anyone receiving property under the will must survive for thirty days (or forty-five or sixty) after the death of the person who made the will. This is so that if the two people die in the same accident there will not be two probates and the property will not go to the other party's heirs.

EXAMPLE
☛ Fred and Wilma were married and each had children by previous marriages. They didn't have survivorship clauses in their wills and they were in an airplane crash and died. Fred's children hired several expert witnesses and a large law firm to prove that at the time of the crash Fred lived for a few minutes longer than Wilma. That way, when Wilma died first, all of her property went to Fred. When he died a few minutes later, all of Fred and Wilma's property went to his children. Wilma's children got nothing.

GUARDIANS

If you have minor children you should name a guardian for them. There are two types of guardians, a guardian over the *person* and a guardian over the *property*. The first is the person who decides where the children will live and makes the other parental decisions for them. A guardian of the property is in charge of the minor's property and inheritance. In most cases, one person is appointed guardian of both the person and property. But some people prefer the children to live with one person, but to have the money held by another person.

EXAMPLE
☛ Sandra was a widow with a young daughter. She knew that if anything happened to her, her sister would be the best person to raise her daughter. But her sister was never good with money. So when Sandra made out her will, she named her sister as guardian over the person of her daughter and she named her father as guardian over the estate of her daughter.

EXAMPLE   When naming a guardian, it is always advisable to name an alternate guardian in case your first choice is unable to serve for any reason.

CHILDREN'S TRUST

When a parent dies leaving a minor child and the child's property is held by a guardian, the guardianship ends when the child reaches the age of eighteen, and all of the property is turned over to the child. Most parents do not feel their children are competent at the age of eighteen to handle large sums of money and prefer that it be held until the child is twenty-one, twenty-five, thirty, or even older.

If you wish to set up a complicated system of determining when your children should receive various amounts of your estate, or if you want the property held to a higher age than thirty-five, you should consult a lawyer to draft a trust. However, if you want a simple provision that the funds be held until they reach a higher age than eighteen, and you have someone you trust to make decisions about paying for education or other expenses for your child or children, you can put that provision in your will as a children's trust.

The children's trust trustee can be the same person as the guardian or a different person. It is advisable to name an alternate trustee if your first choice is unable to handle it.

EXECUTOR

An *executor (executrix* if female) is the person who will be in charge of your probate. He or she will gather your assets, handle the sale of them if necessary, prepare an inventory, hire an attorney, and distribute the property. This should be a person you trust, and if it is, then you can state in your will that no bond will be required to be posted by him or her. Otherwise, the court will require that a surety bond be paid for by your estate to guaranty that the person is honest. You can appoint a bank to handle your estate, but their fees are usually very high.

It is best to appoint a resident of your state, both because it is easier and because a bond may be required of a non-resident even if your will waives it.

Some people like to name two persons to handle their estate to avoid jealousy, or to have them check on each other's honesty. However, this is not a good idea. It makes double work in getting the papers signed, and there can be problems if they cannot agree on something.

The person handling your estate is entitled to compensation. A family member will often waive the fee, but if there is a lot of work involved he or she may request the fee, or other family members may insist that he or she take one. You can insist in your will that your executor is paid a fee.

In Massachusetts, an executor cannot sell real estate without approval by the court unless the power to do so is included in the will. If you trust your executor, you can avoid the expense and delay of this by giving him or her the power to do so without court approval.

Witnesses

A will in Massachusetts, and in all other states except Vermont, must be witnessed by two persons to be valid. Therefore, unless you own property in Vermont, you do not need more than two witnesses.

In Massachusetts (unlike some states), it is legal for a beneficiary of a will to be a witness to the will. However, this is not a good idea, especially if there is anyone who may contest your will.

SELF-PROVING AFFIDAVIT

As mentioned above, a will only needs two witnesses to be legal, but if it includes a self-proving clause and is notarized, the will can be admitted to probate quickly and there is no need to contact the witnesses. If it is not self-proved then one of the witnesses must go to the courthouse and sign a statement that the will is genuine.

In an emergency situation, for example, if you are bedridden and there is no notary available, you can execute your will without the self-proving page. As long as it has two witnesses, it will be valid. The only drawback is that at least one of the witnesses will later have to sign an oath.

DISINHERITING SOMEONE

Because it may result in your will being challenged in court, you should not make your own will if you intend to disinherit someone. However, you may wish to leave one child less than another because you already made a gift to that child, or perhaps that child needs the money less than the other.

If you do give more to one child than to another, then you should state your reasons to show that you thought out your plan. Otherwise, the one who received less might argue that you didn't realize what you were doing and were not competent to make a will.

FUNERAL ARRANGEMENTS

There is no harm in stating your preferences in your will, but in most states, directions for a funeral are not legally enforceable. Often a will is not found until after the funeral. Therefore, it is better to tell your family about your wishes or to make prior arrangements yourself.

HANDWRITTEN WILLS

In some states, a person can hand write a will without any witnesses, and it will be held valid. This is called a *holographic* will. In Massachusetts, however, such a will would not be valid. If the holographic will was executed in another state where such a will is legal, it could effectively pass property in the state of Massachusetts.

FORMS

There are fourteen different will forms included in this book for easy use. You can either cut them out or photocopy them, or you can retype them on plain paper.

The forms in this book are printed on both sides of the page. If you photocopy them on separate pages or type your will on more than one piece of paper, you should staple the pages together, initial each page and have both witnesses initial each page and each page should state at the bottom, "page 1 of 3," "page 2 of 3," etc.

CORRECTIONS

Your will should have no white-outs or erasures. If for some reason it is impossible to make a will without corrections, they should be initialed by you and both witnesses.

One eye-witness is worth more than ten who tell what they have heard.
—Plautus, c. 254 - 184 B.C.

HOW TO EXECUTE YOUR WILL 4

The signing of a will is a serious legal event and must be done properly or the will may be declared invalid. Preferably, it should be done in a private room without distraction. All parties must watch each other sign and no one should leave the scene until all have signed.

EXAMPLE

☛ Ebenezer was bedridden in a small room. His will was brought in to him to sign, but the witnesses could not actually see his hand signing because a dresser was in the way. His will was ignored by the court and his property went to two persons who were not in his will.

PROCEDURE

To be sure your will is valid, you should follow these rules:

☛ You must state to your witnesses: "This is my will. I have read it and I understand it and this is how I want it to read. I want you two (or three) people to be my witnesses." Contrary to popular belief, you do not have to read it to the witnesses or to let them read it.

☛ You must date your will and sign your name at the end in ink exactly as it is printed in the will, and you should initial each page as both witnesses watch.

☛ You and the other witnesses must watch as each witness signs in ink and initials each page.

SELF-PROVING
AFFIDAVIT

As explained in the last chapter, it is important to attach a self-proving affidavit to your will. This means that you will need to have a notary public present to watch everyone sign. If it is impossible to have a notary present, your will will still be valid, but the probate process may be delayed.

After your witnesses have signed as attesting witnesses under your name, you and they should sign the self-proving page and the notary should notarize it. The notary should not be one of your witnesses.

It is a good idea to make at least one copy of your will, but you should not personally sign the copies or have them notarized. The reason for this is if you cancel or destroy your will someone may produce a copy and have it probated, or if you lose or destroy a copy a court may assume you intended to revoke the original.

EXAMPLE

☛ Michael typed out a copy of his will and made two photocopies. He had the original and both copies signed and notarized. He gave the original to his sister who was his executor and kept the two copies. Upon his death the two copies were not found among his papers. Because these copies were in his possession and not found it was assumed that he destroyed them. A court ruled that by destroying them he must have intended to revoke the original will and his property went to persons not listed in his will.

AFTER YOU SIGN YOUR WILL 5

STORING YOUR WILL

Your will should be kept in a place safe from fire and easily accessible to your heirs. Your personal representative should know of its whereabouts. It can be kept in a home safe or fire box.

In some states, the opening of a safe deposit box in a bank after a person's death is a complicated affair, but in Massachusetts a will can be removed from a safe deposit box easily, so you can keep it there.

If you are close to your children and can trust them explicitly, then you could allow one of them to keep the will in his or her safe deposit box. However, if you later decide to limit that child's share there could be a problem.

EXAMPLE

☛ Diane made out her will giving her property to her two children equally and gave it to her older child, Bill, to hold. Years later, Bill moved away and her younger child, Mary, took care of her by coming over every day. Diane made a new will giving most her property to Mary. Upon Diane's death, Bill came to town and found the new will in Diane's house, but he destroyed it and probated the old will which gave him half the property.

REVOKING YOUR WILL

The usual way to revoke a will is to execute a new one that states that it revokes all previously made wills. To revoke a will without making a new one, one can tear, burn, cancel, deface, obliterate, or destroy it, as long as this is done with the intention of revoking it. If this is done accidentally, the will is not legally revoked.

EXAMPLE
☞ Ralph tells his son Clyde to go to the basement safe and tear up his (Ralph's) will. If Clyde does not tear it up in Ralph's presence, it is probably not effectively revoked.

REVIVAL
What if you change your will by drafting a new one, and later decide you don't like the changes and want to go back to your old will? Can you destroy the new one and revive the old one? NO! Once you execute a new will revoking an old will, you cannot revive the old will unless you execute a new document stating that you intend to revive the old will. In other words, you really should execute a new will.

CHANGING YOUR WILL

You should not make any changes on your will after it has been signed. If you cross out a person's name or add a clause to a will that has already been signed, your change will not be valid and your entire will might become invalid.

One way to amend a will is to execute a *codicil*. A codicil is an amendment to a will. However, a codicil must be executed just like a will. It must have the same number of witnesses, and to be self-proved it must include a self-proving page that must be notarized.

Because a codicil requires the same formality as a will, it is usually better to just make a new will.

In an emergency situation, if you want to change something in your will, but cannot get to a notary to have it self-proved, you can execute a codicil which is witnessed, but not self-proved. As long as it is properly witnessed (two witnesses) it will legally change your will. The only drawback would be that the witnesses would have to later sign an oath if it were not self-proved.

To prepare a codicil, use form 18. To self-prove the codicil, use form 19.

Confidence in others' honesty is no light testimony of one's own integrity.
—Michel de Montaigne

How to Make a Living Will 6

No, a living will is not a videotape of a person making a will. It has nothing to do with the usual type of will that distributes property. A living will is a document by which a person declares that he or she does not want artificial life support systems used if he or she becomes terminally ill.

Modern science can often keep a body alive even if the brain is permanently dead, or if the person is in constant pain. In recent years, all states have legalized living wills either by statute or by court decision.

A living will must be signed in front of two witnesses who should not be blood relatives or a spouse. If the person is physically unable to sign, he or she may read the living will out loud and direct one of the witnesses to sign it for him or her.

A sample living will form is included in appendix B of this book as form 20.

Behold, I do not give lectures or a little charity, When I give I give myself.
—Walt Whitman, Leaves of Grass

How to Make Anatomical Gifts 7

Massachusetts residents are allowed to donate their bodies or organs for research or transplantation. Consent may be given by a relative of a deceased person, but because relatives are often in shock or too upset to make such a decision, it is better to have one's intent made clear before death. This can be done by a statement in a will or by another signed document such as a Uniform Donor Card. The gift may be of all or part of one's body, and it may be made to a specific person such as a physician or an ill relative.

The document making the donation must be signed before two witnesses who must also sign in each other's presence. If the donor cannot sign, then the document may be signed for him at his direction in the presence of the witnesses.

The donor may designate in the document who the physician is that will carry out the procedure.

If the document or will has been delivered to a specific donee it may be amended or revoked by the donor in the following ways:

- ☛ By executing and delivering a signed statement to the donee.
- ☛ By an oral statement to two witnesses communicated to the donee.
- ☛ By an oral statement during a terminal illness made to an attending physician and communicated to the donee.

☞ By a signed document found on the person of the donor or in his or her effects.

If a document of gift has not been delivered to a donee it may be revoked by any of the above methods or by destruction, cancellation, or mutilation of the document. It may also be revoked in the same method a will is revoked as described on page 36.

A Uniform Donor Card is included in appendix B as form 21. It must be signed in the presence of two signing witnesses.

Appendix A
Sample Filled-in Forms

The following pages include sample filled-in forms for some of the wills in this book. They are filled out in different ways for different situations. You should look at all of them to see how the different sections can be completed. Only one example of a self-proved will affidavit is shown, but you should use it with every will.

Last Will and Testament

I, _____John Smith_____ a resident of _____Suffolk_____ County, Massachusetts do hereby make, publish, and declare this to be my Last Will and Testament, hereby revoking any and all Wills and Codicils heretofore made by me.

FIRST: I direct that all my just debts and funeral expenses be paid out of my estate as soon after my death as is practicable.

SECOND: I may leave a statement or list disposing of certain items of my tangible personal property. Any such statement or list in existence at the time of my death shall be determinative with respect to all items bequeathed therein.

THIRD: I give, devise, and bequeath all my estate, real, personal, and mixed, of whatever kind and wherever situated, of which I may die seized or possessed, or in which I may have any interest or over which I may have any power of appointment or testamentary disposition, to my spouse, _____Barbara Smith_____. If my said spouse does not survive me, I give, devise, and bequeath the said property to _my sisters, Jan Smith, Joan Smith,_ _and Jennifer Smith in equal shares--_ _--_ _--,_ or the survivor of them.

FOURTH: In the event that any beneficiary fails to survive me by thirty days, then this will shall take effect as if that person had predeceased me.

FIFTH: I hereby nominate, constitute, and appoint _____Barbara Smith_____ as Executor of this, my Last Will and Testament. In the event that such named person is unable or unwilling to serve at any time or for any reason, then I nominate, constitute, and appoint ___my uncle, Reginald Smith,___ as Executor in the place and stead of the person first named herein. It is my will and I direct that my Executor shall not be required to furnish a bond for the faithful performance of his or her duties in any jurisdiction, any provision of law to the contrary notwithstanding, and I give my Executor full power to administer my estate, including the power to settle claims, pay debts, and sell, lease or exchange real and personal property without court order.

IN WITNESS WHEREOF I declare this to be my Last Will and Testament and execute it willingly as my free and voluntary act for the purposes expressed herein and I am of legal age and sound mind and make this under no constraint or undue influence, this _29th_ day of _____January_____, _1999_ at _____Boston_____ Commonwealth of Massachusetts.

_____*John Smith*_____

The foregoing instrument was on said date subscribed at the end thereof by _____John Smith_____, the above named Testator who signed, published, and declared this instrument to be his/her Last Will and Testament in the presence of us and each of us, who thereupon at his/her request, in his/her presence, and in the presence of each other, have hereunto subscribed our names as witnesses thereto. We are of sound mind and proper age to witness a will and understand this to be his/her will, and to the best of our knowledge testator is of legal age to make a will, of sound mind, and under no constraint or undue influence.

_Brenda Jones_____ residing at __Revere, Massachusetts_____

_John Doe_____ residing at __Winthrop, Massachusetts_____

Last Will and Testament

I, _____John Smith_____ a resident of _____Middlesex_____ County, Massachusetts do hereby make, publish, and declare this to be my Last Will and Testament, hereby revoking any and all Wills and Codicils heretofore made by me.

FIRST: I direct that all my just debts and funeral expenses be paid out of my estate as soon after my death as is practicable.

SECOND: I may leave a statement or list disposing of certain items of my tangible personal property. Any such statement or list in existence at the time of my death shall be determinative with respect to all items bequeathed therein.

THIRD: I give, devise, and bequeath all my estate, real, personal, and mixed, of whatever kind and wherever situated, of which I may die seized or possessed, or in which I may have any interest or over which I may have any power of appointment or testamentary disposition, to my spouse, _____Barbara Smith_____. If my said spouse does not survive me, I give, devise, and bequeath the said property to my children ___Amy Smith, Beamy Smith, and Seamy Smith--- --, in equal shares or to their lineal descendants, per stirpes.

FOURTH: In the event that any beneficiary fails to survive me by thirty days, then this will shall take effect as if that person had predeceased me.

FIFTH: I hereby nominate, constitute, and appoint _____Barbara Smith_____ as Excutor of this, my Last Will and Testament. In the event that such named person is unable or unwilling to serve at any time or for any reason, then I nominate, constitute, and appoint my uncle, Reginald Smith, _____ as Executor in the place and stead of the person first named herein. It is my will and I direct that my Executor shall not be required to furnish a bond for the faithful performance of his or her duties in any jurisdiction, any provision of law to the contrary notwithstanding, and I give my Executor full power to administer my estate, including the power to settle claims, pay debts, and sell, lease or exchange real and personal property without court order.

IN WITNESS WHEREOF I declare this to be my Last Will and Testament and execute it willingly as my free and voluntary act for the purposes expressed herein and I am of legal age and sound mind and make this under no constraint or undue influence, this _5th_ day of _January_, _1999_ at _North Reading_ Commonwealth of Massachusetts.

_____*John Smith*_____

The foregoing instrument was on said date subscribed at the end thereof by _____Reginald Smith_____, the above named Testator who signed, published, and declared this instrument to be his/her Last Will and Testament in the presence of us and each of us, who thereupon at his/her request, in his/her presence, and in the presence of each other, have hereunto subscribed our names as witnesses thereto. We are of sound mind and proper age to witness a will and understand this to be his/her will, and to the best of our knowledge testator is of legal age to make a will, of sound mind, and under no constraint or undue influence.

_____*Brenda Jones*_____residing at__Wakefield, Massachusetts__

_____*John Doe*_____residing at__Woburn, Massachusetts__

Last Will and Testament

I, _____John Doe_____ a resident of _____Essex_____ County, Florida do hereby make, publish, and declare this to be my Last Will and Testament, hereby revoking any and all Wills and Codicils heretofore made by me.

FIRST: I direct that all my just debts and funeral expenses be paid out of my estate as soon after my death as is practicable.

SECOND: I may leave a statement or list disposing of certain items of my tangible personal property. Any such statement or list in existence at the time of my death shall be determinative with respect to all items bequeathed therein.

THIRD: I give, devise, and bequeath all my estate, real, personal, and mixed, of whatever kind and wherever situated, of which I may die seized or possessed, or in which I may have any interest or over which I may have any power of appointment or testamentary disposition, to my children _James Doe, Mary Doe, Larry Doe, Barry Doe, Carrie Doe, and Moe Doe----_ --- --- _____, plus any afterborn or adopted children in equal shares or to their lineal descendants per stirpes.

FOURTH: In the event that any beneficiary fails to survive me by thirty days, then this will shall take effect as if that person had predeceased me.

FIFTH: In the event any of my children have not attained the age of 18 years at the time of my death, I hereby nominate, constitute, and appoint _____Herbert Doe_____ as guardian over the person of any of my children who have not reached the age of majority at the time of my death. In the event that said guardian is unable or unwilling to serve, then I nominate, constitute, and appoint _____Tom Doe_____ as guardian. Said guardian shall serve without bond or surety.

SIXTH: In the event any of my children have not attained the age of 18 years at the time of my death, I hereby nominate, constitute, and appoint _____Herbert Doe_____ as guardian over the property of any of my children who have not reached the age of majority at the time of my death. In the event that said guardian is unable or unwilling to serve, then I nominate, constitute, and appoint _____Tom Doe_____ as guardian. Said guardian shall serve without bond or surety.

SEVENTH: I hereby nominate, constitute, and appoint _____Clarence Doe_____ as Executor of this, my Last Will and Testament. In the event that such named person is unable or unwilling to serve at any time or for any reason, then I nominate, constitute, and appoint _____Englebert Doe_____ as Executor in the place and stead of the person first named herein. It is my will and I direct that my Executor shall not be required to furnish a bond for the faithful performance of his or her duties in any jurisdiction, any provision of law to the contrary notwithstanding, and I give my Executor full power to administer my estate, including the power to settle claims, pay debts, and sell, lease or exchange real and personal property without court order.

IN WITNESS WHEREOF I declare this to be my Last Will and Testament and execute it willingly as my free and voluntary act for the purposes expressed herein and I am of legal age and sound mind and make this under no constraint or undue influence, this __2nd__ day of ___July___, __2001__ at __North Andover__ Commonwealth of Massachusetts.

_____John Doe_____

The foregoing instrument was on said date subscribed at the end thereof by _____John Doe_____, the above named Testator who signed, published, and declared this instrument to be his/her Last Will and Testament in the presence of us and each of us, who thereupon at his/her request, in his/her presence, and in the presence of each other, have hereunto subscribed our names as witnesses thereto. We are of sound mind and proper age to witness a will and understand this to be his/her will, and to the best of our knowledge testator is of legal age to make a will, of sound mind, and under no constraint or undue influence.

_____Jane Roe_____residing at__Topsfield, Massachusetts___

_____Melvin Coe_____residing at__Marblehead, Massachusetts___

Last Will and Testament

I, _____Mary Smith_____ a resident of _Hampden_____ County, Florida do hereby make, publish, and declare this to be my Last Will and Testament, hereby revoking any and all Wills and Codicils heretofore made by me.

FIRST: I direct that all my just debts and funeral expenses be paid out of my estate as soon after my death as is practicable.

SECOND: I may leave a statement or list disposing of certain items of my tangible personal property. Any such statement or list in existence at the time of my death shall be determinative with respect to all items bequeathed therein.

THIRD: I give, devise, and bequeath all my estate, real, personal, and mixed, of whatever kind and wherever situated, of which I may die seized or possessed, or in which I may have any interest or over which I may have any power of appointment or testamentary disposition, to the following: my brothers John Smith and James Smith, in equal shares---------------- --- --- --, or to the survivor of them.

FOURTH: In the event that any beneficiary fails to survive me by thirty days, then this will shall take effect as if that person had predeceased me.

FIFTH: I hereby nominate, constitute, and appoint _____Herbert Doe_____ as Executor of this, my Last Will and Testament. In the event that such named person is unable or unwilling to serve at any time or for any reason, then I nominate, constitute, and appoint _____Tom Doe_____ as Executor in the place and stead of the person first named herein. It is my will and I direct that my Executor shall not be required to furnish a bond for the faithful performance of his or her duties in any jurisdiction, any provision of law to the contrary notwithstanding, and I give my Executor full power to administer my estate, including the power to settle claims, pay debts, and sell, lease or exchange real and personal property without court order.

IN WITNESS WHEREOF I declare this to be my Last Will and Testament and execute it willingly as my free and voluntary act for the purposes expressed herein and I am of legal age and sound mind and make this under no constraint or undue influence, this _6th_ day of ____May_____, _2002__ at _____Springfield_____ Commonwealth of Massachusetts.

Mary Smith
_____

The foregoing instrument was on said date subscribed at the end thereof by _____Mary Smith_____, the above named Testator who signed, published, and declared this instrument to be his/her Last Will and Testament in the presence of us and each of us, who thereupon at his/her request, in his/her presence, and in the presence of each other, have hereunto subscribed our names as witnesses thereto. We are of sound mind and proper age to witness a will and understand this to be his/her will, and to the best of our knowledge testator is of legal age to make a will, of sound mind, and under no constraint or undue influence.

_____Leon Brown_____residing at_____Holyoke, Massachusetts_____

_____Mildred Brown_____residing at_____Chicopee, Massachusetts____

Self-Proved Will Affidavit
(attach to Will)

COMMONWEALTH OF MASSACHUSETTS

COUNTY OF _____Hampshire_____

    I, the undersigned, an officer authorized to administer oaths, certify that
_____John Doe_____, the testator and
___Jane Roe_____, and ____Melvin Coe_____,
the witnesses, whose names are signed to the attached or foregoing instrument and whose signatures appear below, having appeared before me and having been first been duly sworn, each then declared to me that: 1) the attached or foregoing instrument is the last will of the testator; 2) the testator willingly and voluntarily declared, signed, and executed the will in the presence of the witnesses; 3) the witnesses signed the will upon the request of the testator, in the presence and hearing of the testator and in the presence of each other; 4) to the best knowledge of each witness, the testator was, at the time of signing, of the age of majority (or otherwise legally competent to make a will), of sound mind and memory, and under no constraint or undue influence; and 5) each witness was and is competent and of proper age to witness a will.

_____*John Doe*_____ (Testator)

_____*Jane Roe*_____ (Witness)

_____*Melvin Coe*_____ (Witness)

Subscribed and sworn to before me by _____John Doe_____, the testator, who is personally known to me or who has produced ___MA.Dr. Lic. D1234567890___ as identification, and by ___Jane Roe_____, a witness, who is personally known to me or who has produced ___MA.Dr. Lic. R9876543210___ as identification, and by ___Melvin Coe_____, a witness, who is personally known to me or who has produced ___MA.Dr. Lic. C4567890123___ as identification, this __5th__ day of_____July_____, __2001__.

_____*C.U. Sine*_____
Notary or other officer

Codicil to the Will of

_____ Larry Lowe _____

I, _____ Larry Lowe _____, a resident of _____ Nantucket _____ County, Massachusetts declare this to be the first codicil to my Last Will and Testament dated _____ July 5 _____, __1999__.

FIRST: I hereby revoke the clause of my Will which reads as follows: FOURTH: I hereby leave $5000.00 to my daughter Mildred-----------------------
----

--.

SECOND: I hereby add the following clause to my Will: _____ FOURTH: I hereby leave $1000.00 to my daughter Mildred-----------------------
----

--.

THIRD: In all other respects I hereby confirm and republish my Last Will and Testament dated _____ July 5 _____, __1999__.

IN WITNESS WHEREOF, I have signed, published, and declared the foregoing instrument as and for a codicil to my Last Will and Testament, this __5th__ day of _____ January _____, __2000__.

_____ _Larry Lowe_ _____

The foregoing instrument was on the __5th__ day of _____ January _____, __2000__, signed at the end thereof, and at the same time published and declared by _____ Larry Lowe _____, as and for a codicil to his/her Last Will and Testament, dated _____ July 5 _____, __1999__, in the presence of each of us, who, this attestation clause having been read to us, did at the request of the said testator/testatrix, in his/her presence and in the presence of each other signed our names as witnesses thereto.

James Smith _____residing at___ Nantucket, Massachusetts _____

Mary Smith _____residing at___ Nantucket, Massachusetts _____

Living Will and Health Care Proxy of

<u>   Christopher Jackson   </u>

ARTICLE I: LIVING WILL

KNOW ALL MEN BY THESE PRESENTS: That I, <u>   Christopher Jackson   </u>, of <u>   Brookline   </u>, Commonwealth of Massachusetts, do hereby make, publish and declare ARTICLE I of this instrument to be my Living Will. This Living Will shall have no effect upon, and shall not revoke or cancel, any other wills, codicils or testamentary dispositions heretofore made by me. This Living Will shall also have no effect on the validity of my Health Care Proxy contained in Article II of this Instrument.

A. If my death cannot be avoided, and if I have lost the ability to interact with others and have no reasonable chance of regaining this ability, or if my suffering is intense and irreversible, I wish to have the following expressions of my desire respected and acted upon by the individuals mentioned hereinbelow:

1. I do not want to have my life prolonged.

2. I would not wish to have life support from mechanical devices or other life prolonging procedures.

Notwithstanding the foregoing, I would want to have care that gives comfort and support and that facilitates my interaction with others to the extent that is possible and which brings peace.

B. I do not fear death itself as much as the indignities of deterioration, dependence and hopeless pain. I therefore ask that medication be mercifully administered to me to alleviate suffering, even though so doing may hasten the moment of death.

ARTICLE II: HEALTH CARE PROXY

KNOW ALL MEN BY THESE PRESENTS: That I, <u>   Christopher Jackson   </u> (hereinafter also the "Principal"), a legal resident of <u>   Brookline   </u>, Commonwealth of Massachusetts, do hereby make, publish and declare ARTICLE II of this instrument to be my HEALTH CARE PROXY and by these presents in ARTICLE II do make, constitute and appoint <u>   Debra Jackson   </u> of <u>   Brookline   </u>, Massachusetts my true and lawful health care agent (hereinafter the "Agent") and do hereby grant said Agent authority to make health care decisions on my behalf, said authority taking effort upon a determination, pursuant to the provisions of ARTICLE II Sections (A) and (B) below, that I lack the capacity to make or to communicate such health care decisions. It is my intention herein to appoint a health care agent and to create a valid and binding HEALTH CARE PROXY pursuant to Massachusetts General Laws ch. 201D and to comply with the provisions thereunder.

A. The determination that I lack the capacity to make or to communicate health care decisions shall be made in writing by the attending physician according to accepted standards of medical judgment and shall contain said attending physician's opinion regarding the cause and nature of my incapacity as well as the extent and probable duration of such incapacity.

B. If the attending physician determines that I have the capacity to make or to communicate health care decisions: 1) the authority of the Agent shall cease; and 2) my consent for treatment shall be required.

C. The Agent shall have the authority, pursuant to the provisions of this HEALTH CARE PROXY, to make any and all health care decisions on my behalf including decisions about life sustaining treatment after an independent doctor concurs with my physician that there is no chance of my recovery. The Agent may look to my Living Will in Article I of this instrument for guidance in making such health care decisions provided that the Agent's sole interpretation of my Living Will shall be binding and conclusive on all persons.

D. I request that health care providers comply with the Agent's health care decisions to the same extent as if I had made such decisions.

E. No health care provider or employee thereof shall be subject to criminal or civil liability or be deemed to have engaged in unprofessional conduct, for carrying out in good faith the Agent's health care decisions pursuant to this HEALTH CARE PROXY.

F. No person acting as Agent pursuant to this HEALTH CARE PROXY shall be subject to criminal or civil liability for making a health care decision pursuant to this HEALTH CARE PROXY.

G. In the event that my Agent, _____Debra Jackson_____, shall be unavailable or shall for any reason, including removal, death, incapacity or resignation, cease to serve or fail to qualify as Agent hereunder, then I designate my father, _____James Jackson_____, now or formerly of _____Quincy_____, _____Massachusetts_____ to serve as alternate Agent with full power and authority thereunder.

H. In the event that any one or more of the provisions contained in this instrument shall for any reason be held to be invalid, illegal, or unenforceable in any respect, such validity, illegality or unenforceability shall not affect the validity, legality, or enforceability of any of the other provisions of this instrument.

IN WITNESS WHEREOF, I, Christopher Jackson, do hereto set my hand and in the presence of the Witnesses publish and declare this Instrument, typewritten on this page and 1 other preceding sheet, one side only being used, and the preceding page having been initialed by me, to be my LIVING WILL and HEALTH CARE PROXY this _1st_ day of _____May_____, _2000_.

_____*Christopher Jackson*_____
_____Christopher Jackson_____, Principal

Signed, sealed, published and declared by _Christopher Jackson_, as for, and acknowledged by _Christopher Jackson_ to be his Living Will and Health Care Proxy, in the presence of the undersigned, who at his request, in his presence and in the presence of each other, have hereunto subscribed our names as Witnesses the day and year first written above and hereby affirm that each of us is at least eighteen (18) years of age and that the principal appeared to be at least eighteen (18) years of age, of sound mind and under no constraint or undue influence.

_____*Lucille Witness*_____ of _____Wrentham, MA._____
_____Lucille Witness_____

_____*Joseph Witness*_____ of _____Wrentham, MA._____
_____Joseph Witness_____

COMMONWEALTH OF MASSACHUSETTS

Middlesex, SS   Date: _____May 1, 2000_____

Then personally appeared the above _Christopher Jackson_, and acknowledged the foregoing instrument to be his free act and deed before me,

_____*Salvatore Jones*_____
_____Salvatore Jones_____, Notary Public
My Commission Expires: _2/2/01_

APPENDIX B
FORMS

The following pages contain forms that can be used to prepare a will, codicil, living will, and Uniform Donor Card. They should only be used by persons who have read this book, who do not have any complications in their legal affairs and who understand the forms they are using. The forms may be used right out of the book or they may be photocopied or retyped. Two copies of each form are included.

Form 1. Asset and Beneficiary List—*Use this form to keep an accurate record of your estate as well as your beneficiaries' names and addresses.*

Form 2. Preferences and Information List—*Use this form to let your family know of your wishes on matters not usually included in a will.*

Form 3. Simple Will—Spouse and Minor Children—One Guardian. *Use this will if you have minor children and want all your property to go to your spouse, but if your spouse dies previously, then to your minor children. It provides for one person to be guardian over your children and their estates.*

Form 4. Simple Will—Spouse and Minor Children—Two Guardians. *Use this will if you have minor children and want all your property to go to your spouse, but if your spouse dies previously, then to your minor children. It provides for two guardians, one over your children and one over their estates.*

Form 5. Simple Will—Spouse and Minor Children—Guardian and Trust. *This will should be used if you have minor children and want all your property to go to your spouse, but if your spouse dies previously, then to your minor children. It provides for one person to be guardian over your children and for either the same person or another to be trustee over their property. This will allows* *your children's property to be held until they are older than 18 rather than distributing it all to them at age 18.*

Form 6. Simple Will—Spouse and No Children. *Use this will if you want your property to go to your spouse but if your spouse predeceases you, to others or the* **survivor** *of the others.*

Form 7. Simple Will—Spouse and No Children. *Use this will if you want your property to go to your spouse but if your spouse predeceases you, to others or the* **descendants** *of the others.*

Form 8. Simple Will—Spouse and Adult Children. *Use this will if you want all of your property to go to your spouse, but if your spouse dies previously, then to your children, all of whom are adults.*

Form 9. Simple Will—Spouse and Adult Children. *Use this will if you want some of your property to go to your spouse, and some of your property to your children, all of whom are adults.*

Form 10. Simple Will—No Spouse—Minor Children—One Guardian. *Use this will if you do not have a spouse and want all your property to go to your children, at least one of whom is a minor. It provides for one person to be guardian over your children and their estates.*

Form 11. Simple Will—No Spouse—Minor Children—Two Guardians. *Use this will if you do not have a spouse and want all your property to go to your children, at least one of whom is a minor. It provides for two guardians, one over your children and one over their estates.*

Form 12. Simple Will—No Spouse—Minor Children—Guardian and Trust. *Use this will if you do not have a spouse and want all your property to go to your children, at least one of whom is a minor. It provides for one person to be guardian over your children and for either that person or another to be trustee over their property. This will allows your children's property to be held until they are older than 18 rather than distributing it all to them at age 18.*

Form 13. Simple Will—No Spouse—Adult Children. *This will should be used if you wish to leave your property to your adult children, or equally to each* **family** *if they predecease you.*

Form 14. Simple Will—No Spouse—Adult Children. *This will should be used if you wish to leave your property to your adult children, or equally to each* **person** *if they predecease you.*

Form 15. Simple Will—No Spouse and No Children. *Use this will if you have no spouse or children and want your property to go to the* **survivor** *of the people you name.*

Form 16. Simple Will—No Spouse and No Children. *Use this will if you have no spouse or children and want your property to go to the* **descendants** *of the people you name.*

Form 17. Self-Proved Will Affidavit. *This page should be attached to every will as the last page. It must be witnessed and notarized.*

Form 18. Codicil to Will. *This form can be used to change one section of your will. Usually it is just as easy to execute a new will, since all of the same formalities are required.*

Form 19. Self-Proved Codicil Page. *If you decided to execute a codicil instead of making a new will, this page should be attached to your codicil as the last page. It must be witnessed and notarized.*

Form 20. Living Will. *This is a document which expresses your desire to withhold certain extra-ordinary medical treatment should you have a terminal illness and you reach such a state that your wishes to withhold such treatment cannot be determined.*

Form 21. Organ Donor Card. *This form is used to spell out your wishes for donation of your body or any organs.*

HOW TO PICK THE RIGHT WILL

Follow the chart and use the form number in the black circle,
then use form 17, the self-proving affidavit.

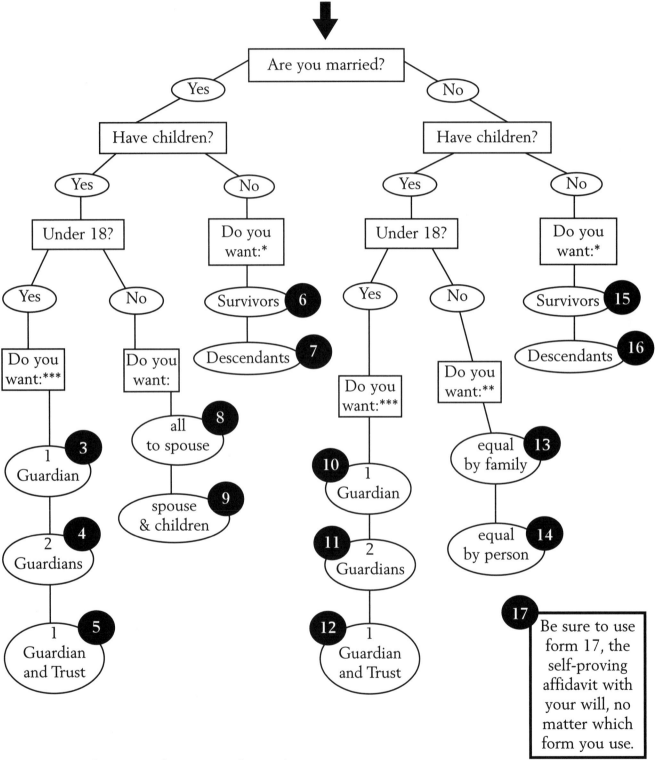

*For an explanation of survivors/descendants, see page 26.
**For an explanation of families/persons, see page 26.
***For an explanation of children's guardians and trust, see pages 28-29

Asset and Beneficiary List

Property Inventory

Assets

Bank Accounts (checking, savings, certificates of deposit)

_____

_____

_____

_____

_____

_____

_____

_____

Real Estate

_____

_____

_____

_____

_____

_____

_____

_____

Vehicles (cars, trucks, boats, planes, RVs, etc.)

_____

_____

_____

_____

_____

_____

_____

_____

Personal Property (collections, jewelry, tools, artwork, household items, etc.)

_____

_____

_____

_____

_____

_____

_____

_____

_____

_____

_____

_____

_____

Stocks/Bonds/Mutual Funds

_____

_____

_____

_____

_____

_____

_____

_____

_____

_____

_____

_____

_____

Retirement Accounts (IRAs, 401(k)s, pension plans, etc.)

_____

_____

_____

_____

_____

_____

Receivables (mortgages held, notes, accounts receivable, personal loans)

_____

_____

_____

_____

_____

_____

Life Insurance

_____
_____
_____
_____
_____
_____
_____

Other Property (trusts, partnerships, businesses, profit sharing, copyrights, etc.)

_____
_____
_____
_____
_____
_____
_____

Liabilities

Real Estate Loans

_____
_____
_____
_____
_____
_____

Vehicle Loans

_____
_____
_____
_____
_____
_____
_____

Other Secured Loans

_____
_____
_____
_____
_____
_____
_____
_____

Unsecured Loans and Debts (taxes, child support, judgments, etc.)

_____
_____
_____
_____
_____
_____
_____

Beneficiary List

Name_____ Address_____ Phone_____

_____
_____
_____
_____
_____
_____
_____

Preferences and Information List

STATEMENT OF DESIRES AND LOCATION OF PROPERTY & DOCUMENTS

I, _____, am signing this document as the expression of my desires as to the matters stated below, and to inform my family members or other significant persons of the location of certain property and documents in the event of any emergency or of my death.

1.   **Funeral Desires.** It is my desire that the following arrangements be made for my funeral and disposition of remains in the event of my death (state if you have made any arrangements, such as pre-paid burial plans, cemetery plots owned, etc.):

❑   Burial at _____
_____.

❑   Cremation at _____
_____.

❑   Other specific desires: _____
_____
_____.

2.   **Pets.** I have the following pet(s): _____
_____. The following are my desires concerning the care of said pet(s): _____
_____
_____.

4.   **Notification.** I would like the following person(s) notified in the event of emergency or death (give name, address and phone number):

_____
_____
_____
_____
_____.

5.   **Location of Documents.** The following is a list of important documents, and their location:

❑   Last Will and Testament, dated _____. Location: _____
_____.

❑   Durable Power of Attorney, dated _____. Location: _____
_____.

❑   Living Will, dated _____. Location: _____
_____.

❑   Deed(s) to real estate (describe property location and location of deed):

_____
_____
_____

65

❏ Title(s) to vehicles (cars, boats, etc.) (Describe vehicle, its location, and location of title, registration, or other documents):

_____
_____
_____
_____

❏ Life insurance policies (list name address & phone number of insurance company and insurance agent, policy number, and location of policy):

_____
_____
_____

❏ Other insurance policies (list type, company & agent, policy number, and location of policy):

_____
_____
_____

❏ Other: (list other documents such as stock certificates, bonds, certificates of deposit, etc., and their location):

_____
_____
_____

6.   **Location of Assets.** In addition to items readily visible in my home or listed above, I have the following assets:

❏ Safe deposit box located at _____, box number _____. Key located at: _____.

❏ Bank accounts (list name & address of bank, type of account, and account number):

_____

❏ Other (describe the item and give its location):

_____
_____
_____
_____
_____

7.   Other desires or information (state any desires or provide any information not given above; use additional sheets of paper if necessary):

_____
_____
_____
_____
_____

Dated: _____

_____

Signature

Last Will and Testament

I, _____ a resident of _____
County, Massachusetts do hereby make, publish, and declare this to be my Last Will and Testament, hereby revoking any and all Wills and Codicils heretofore made by me.

FIRST: I direct that all my just debts and funeral expenses be paid out of my estate as soon after my death as is practicable.

SECOND: I may leave a statement or list disposing of certain items of my tangible personal property. Any such statement or list in existence at the time of my death shall be determinative with respect to all items bequeathed therein.

THIRD: I give, devise, and bequeath all my estate, real, personal, and mixed, of whatever kind and wherever situated, of which I may die seized or possessed, or in which I may have any interest or over which I may have any power of appointment or testamentary disposition, to my spouse, _____. If my said spouse does not survive me, I give, and bequeath the said property to my children _____
_____
_____,
plus any afterborn or adopted children in equal shares or their lineal descendants, per stirpes.

FOURTH: In the event that any beneficiary fails to survive me by thirty days, then this will shall take effect as if that person had predeceased me.

FIFTH: Should my spouse not survive me, I hereby nominate, constitute, and appoint _____ as guardian over the person and estate of any of my children who have not reached the age of majority at the time of my death. In the event that said guardian is unable or unwilling to serve, then I nominate, constitute, and appoint _____ as guardian. Said guardian shall serve without bond or surety.

SIXTH: I hereby nominate, constitute, and appoint _____ as Executor of this, my Last Will and Testament. In the event that such named person is unable or unwilling to serve at any time or for any reason, then I nominate, constitute, and appoint _____ as Executor in the place and stead of the person first named herein. It is my will and I direct that my Executor shall not be required to furnish a bond for the faithful performance of his or her duties in any jurisdiction, any provision of law to the contrary notwithstanding, and I give my Executor full power to administer my estate, including the power to settle claims, pay debts, and sell, lease or exchange real and personal property without court order.

IN WITNESS WHEREOF I declare this to be my Last Will and Testament and execute it willingly as my free and voluntary act for the purposes expressed herein and I am of legal age and sound mind and make this under no constraint or undue influence, this _____ day of _____, _____ at _____ Commonwealth of Massachusetts.

_____

The foregoing instrument was on said date subscribed at the end thereof by _____, the above named Testator who signed, published, and declared this instrument to be his/her Last Will and Testament in the presence of us and each of us, who thereupon at his/her request, in his/her presence, and in the presence of each other, have hereunto subscribed our names as witnesses thereto. We are of sound mind and proper age to witness a will and understand this to be his/her will, and to the best of our knowledge testator is of legal age to make a will, of sound mind, and under no constraint or undue influence.

_____residing at_____

_____residing at_____

Last Will and Testament

I, _____ a resident of _____
County, Massachusetts do hereby make, publish, and declare this to be my Last Will and Testament, hereby revoking any and all Wills and Codicils heretofore made by me.

FIRST: I direct that all my just debts and funeral expenses be paid out of my estate as soon after my death as is practicable.

SECOND: I may leave a statement or list disposing of certain items of my tangible personal property. Any such statement or list in existence at the time of my death shall be determinative with respect to all items bequeathed therein.

THIRD: I give, devise, and bequeath all my estate, real, personal, and mixed, of whatever kind and wherever situated, of which I may die seized or possessed, or in which I may have any interest or over which I may have any power of appointment or testamentary disposition, to my spouse, _____. If my said spouse does not survive me, I give, and bequeath the said property to my children _____
_____
_____,
plus any afterborn or adopted children in equal shares or their lineal descendants, per stirpes.

FOURTH: In the event that any beneficiary fails to survive me by thirty days, then this will shall take effect as if that person had predeceased me.

FIFTH: Should my spouse not survive me, I hereby nominate, constitute, and appoint _____, as guardian over the person of any of my children who have not reached the age of majority at the time of my death. In the event that said guardian is unable or unwilling to serve, then I nominate, constitute, and appoint _____ as guardian. Said guardian shall serve without bond or surety.

SIXTH: Should my spouse not survive me, I hereby nominate, constitute, and appoint _____ as guardian over the estate of any of my children who have not reached the age of majority at the time of my death. In the event that said guardian is unable or unwilling to serve, then I nominate, constitute, and appoint _____ as guardian. Said guardian shall serve without bond or surety.

SEVENTH: I hereby nominate, constitute, and appoint _____ as Executor of this, my Last Will and Testament. In the event that such named person is unable or unwilling to serve at any time or for any reason, then I nominate, constitute, and appoint _____ as Executor in the place and stead of the person first named herein. It is my will and I direct that my Executor shall not be required to furnish a bond for the faithful performance of his or her duties in any jurisdiction, any provision of law to the contrary notwithstanding, and I give my Executor full power to administer my estate, including the power to settle claims, pay debts, and sell, lease or exchange real and personal property without court order.

IN WITNESS WHEREOF I declare this to be my Last Will and Testament and execute it willingly as my free and voluntary act for the purposes expressed herein and I am of legal age and sound mind and make this under no constraint or undue influence, this _____ day of _____, _____ at _____ Commonwealth of Massachusetts.

_____

The foregoing instrument was on said date subscribed at the end thereof by _____, the above named Testator who signed, published, and declared this instrument to be his/her Last Will and Testament in the presence of us and each of us, who thereupon at his/her request, in his/her presence, and in the presence of each other, have hereunto subscribed our names as witnesses thereto. We are of sound mind and proper age to witness a will and understand this to be his/her will, and to the best of our knowledge testator is of legal age to make a will, of sound mind, and under no constraint or undue influence.

_____residing at_____

_____residing at_____

Last Will and Testament

I, _____ a resident of _____ County, Massachusetts do hereby make, publish, and declare this to be my Last Will and Testament, hereby revoking any and all Wills and Codicils heretofore made by me.

FIRST: I direct that all my just debts and funeral expenses be paid out of my estate as soon after my death as is practicable.

SECOND: I may leave a statement or list disposing of certain items of my tangible personal property. Any such statement or list in existence at the time of my death shall be determinative with respect to all items bequeathed therein.

THIRD: I give, devise, and bequeath all my estate, real, personal, and mixed, of whatever kind and wherever situated, of which I may die seized or possessed, or in which I may have any interest or over which I may have any power of appointment or testamentary disposition, to my spouse, _____. If my said spouse does not survive me, I give, and bequeath the said property to my children _____ _____ _____, plus any afterborn or adopted children in equal shares or their lineal descendants, per stirpes.

FOURTH: In the event that any beneficiary fails to survive me by thirty days, then this will shall take effect as if that person had predeceased me.

FIFTH: In the event that any of my children have not reached the age of _____ years at the time of my death, then the share of any such child shall be held in a separate trust by _____ for such child.

The trustee shall use the income and that part of the principal of the trust as is, in the trustee's sole discretion, necessary or desirable to provide proper housing, medical care, food, clothing, entertainment and education for the trust beneficiary, considering the beneficiary's other resources. Any income that is not distributed shall be added to the principal. Additionally, the trustee shall have all powers conferred by the law of the state having jurisdiction over this trust, as well as the power to pay from the assets of the trust reasonable fees necessary to administer the trust.

The trust shall terminate when the child reaches the age specified above and the remaining assets distributed to the child, unless they have been exhausted sooner. In the event the child dies prior to the termination of the trust, then the assets shall pass to the estate of the child. The interests of the beneficiary under this trust shall not be assignable and shall be free from the claims of creditors to the full extent allowed by law.

In the event the said trustee is unable or unwilling to serve for any reason, then I nominate, constitute, and appoint _____as alternate trustee. No bond shall be required of either trustee in any jurisdiction and this trust shall be administered without court supervision as allowed by law.

SIXTH: Should my spouse not survive me, I hereby nominate, constitute, and appoint _____as guardian over the person and estate of any of my children who have not reached the age of majority at the time of my death. In the event that said guardian is unable or unwilling to serve, then I nominate, constitute, and appoint _____ as guardian.

SEVENTH: I hereby nominate, constitute, and appoint _____ as Executor of this, my Last Will and Testament. In the event that such named person is unable or unwilling to serve at any time or for any reason, then I nominate, constitute, and appoint _____ as Executor in the place and stead of the person first named herein. It is my will and I direct that my Executor shall not be required to furnish a bond for the faithful performance of his or her duties in any jurisdiction, any provision of law to the contrary notwithstanding, and I give my Executor full power to administer my estate, including the power to settle claims, pay debts, and sell, lease or exchange real and personal property without court order.

IN WITNESS WHEREOF I declare this to be my Last Will and Testament and execute it willingly as my free and voluntary act for the purposes expressed herein and I am of legal age and sound mind and make this under no constraint or undue influence, this _____ day of _____, _____ at _____ Commonwealth of Massachusetts.

_____

The foregoing instrument was on said date subscribed at the end thereof by _____, the above named Testator who signed, published, and declared this instrument to be his/her Last Will and Testament in the presence of us and each of us, who thereupon at his/her request, in his/her presence, and in the presence of each other, have hereunto subscribed our names as witnesses thereto. We are of sound mind and proper age to witness a will and understand this to be his/her will, and to the best of our knowledge testator is of legal age to make a will, of sound mind, and under no constraint or undue influence.

_____residing at_____

_____residing at_____

Last Will and Testament

I, _____ a resident of _____
County, Massachusetts do hereby make, publish, and declare this to be my Last Will and Testament, hereby revoking any and all Wills and Codicils heretofore made by me.

FIRST: I direct that all my just debts and funeral expenses be paid out of my estate as soon after my death as is practicable.

SECOND: I may leave a statement or list disposing of certain items of my tangible personal property. Any such statement or list in existence at the time of my death shall be determinative with respect to all items bequeathed therein.

THIRD: I give, devise, and bequeath all my estate, real, personal, and mixed, of whatever kind and wherever situated, of which I may die seized or possessed, or in which I may have any interest or over which I may have any power of appointment or testamentary disposition, to my spouse, _____. If my said spouse does not survive me, I give, devise, and bequeath the said property to _____
_____
_____
_____,
or the survivor of them.

FOURTH: In the event that any beneficiary fails to survive me by thirty days, then this will shall take effect as if that person had predeceased me.

FIFTH: I hereby nominate, constitute, and appoint _____ as Executor of this, my Last Will and Testament. In the event that such named person is unable or unwilling to serve at any time or for any reason, then I nominate, constitute, and appoint _____ as Executor in the place and stead of the person first named herein. It is my will and I direct that my Executor shall not be required to furnish a bond for the faithful performance of his or her duties in any jurisdiction, any provision of law to the contrary notwithstanding, and I give my Executor full power to administer my estate, including the power to settle claims, pay debts, and sell, lease or exchange real and personal property without court order.

IN WITNESS WHEREOF I declare this to be my Last Will and Testament and execute it willingly as my free and voluntary act for the purposes expressed herein and I am of legal age and sound mind and make this under no constraint or undue influence, this _____ day of _____, _____ at _____ Commonwealth of Massachusetts.

_____

The foregoing instrument was on said date subscribed at the end thereof by
_____, the above named Testator who signed, published, and declared this instrument to be his/her Last Will and Testament in the presence of us and each of us, who thereupon at his/her request, in his/her presence, and in the presence of each other, have hereunto subscribed our names as witnesses thereto. We are of sound mind and proper age to witness a will and understand this to be his/her will, and to the best of our knowledge testator is of legal age to make a will, of sound mind, and under no constraint or undue influence.

_____residing at_____

_____residing at_____

Last Will and Testament

I, _____ a resident of _____ County, Massachusetts do hereby make, publish, and declare this to be my Last Will and Testament, hereby revoking any and all Wills and Codicils heretofore made by me.

FIRST: I direct that all my just debts and funeral expenses be paid out of my estate as soon after my death as is practicable.

SECOND: I may leave a statement or list disposing of certain items of my tangible personal property. Any such statement or list in existence at the time of my death shall be determinative with respect to all items bequeathed therein.

THIRD: I give, devise, and bequeath all my estate, real, personal, and mixed, of whatever kind and wherever situated, of which I may die seized or possessed, or in which I may have any interest or over which I may have any power of appointment or testamentary disposition, to my spouse, _____. If my said spouse does not survive me, I give, devise, and bequeath the said property to _____ _____ _____ _____, or to their lineal descendants, per stirpes.

FOURTH: In the event that any beneficiary fails to survive me by thirty days, then this will shall take effect as if that person had predeceased me.

FIFTH: I hereby nominate, constitute, and appoint _____ as Executor of this, my Last Will and Testament. In the event that such named person is unable or unwilling to serve at any time or for any reason, then I nominate, constitute, and appoint _____ as Executor in the place and stead of the person first named herein. It is my will and I direct that my Executor shall not be required to furnish a bond for the faithful performance of his or her duties in any jurisdiction, any provision of law to the contrary notwithstanding, and I give my Executor full power to administer my estate, including the power to settle claims, pay debts, and sell, lease or exchange real and personal property without court order.

IN WITNESS WHEREOF I declare this to be my Last Will and Testament and execute it willingly as my free and voluntary act for the purposes expressed herein and I am of legal age and sound mind and make this under no constraint or undue influence, this _____ day of _____, _____ at _____ Commonwealth of Massachusetts.

_____

The foregoing instrument was on said date subscribed at the end thereof by _____, the above named Testator who signed, published, and declared this instrument to be his/her Last Will and Testament in the presence of us and each of us, who thereupon at his/her request, in his/her presence, and in the presence of each other, have hereunto subscribed our names as witnesses thereto. We are of sound mind and proper age to witness a will and understand this to be his/her will, and to the best of our knowledge testator is of legal age to make a will, of sound mind, and under no constraint or undue influence.

_____residing at_____

_____residing at_____

Last Will and Testament

I, _____ a resident of _____ County, Massachusetts do hereby make, publish, and declare this to be my Last Will and Testament, hereby revoking any and all Wills and Codicils heretofore made by me.

FIRST: I direct that all my just debts and funeral expenses be paid out of my estate as soon after my death as is practicable.

SECOND: I may leave a statement or list disposing of certain items of my tangible personal property. Any such statement or list in existence at the time of my death shall be determinative with respect to all items bequeathed therein.

THIRD: I give, devise, and bequeath all my estate, real, personal, and mixed, of whatever kind and wherever situated, of which I may die seized or possessed, or in which I may have any interest or over which I may have any power of appointment or testamentary disposition, to my spouse, _____. If my said spouse does not survive me, I give, devise, and bequeath the said property to my children _____

_____

_____

_____,

in equal shares or to their lineal descendants, per stirpes.

FOURTH: In the event that any beneficiary fails to survive me by thirty days, then this will shall take effect as if that person had predeceased me.

FIFTH: I hereby nominate, constitute, and appoint _____ as Executor of this, my Last Will and Testament. In the event that such named person is unable or unwilling to serve at any time or for any reason, then I nominate, constitute, and appoint _____ as Executor in the place and stead of the person first named herein. It is my will and I direct that my Executor shall not be required to furnish a bond for the faithful performance of his or her duties in any jurisdiction, any provision of law to the contrary notwithstanding, and I give my Executor full power to administer my estate, including the power to settle claims, pay debts, and sell, lease or exchange real and personal property without court order.

IN WITNESS WHEREOF I declare this to be my Last Will and Testament and execute it willingly as my free and voluntary act for the purposes expressed herein and I am of legal age and sound mind and make this under no constraint or undue influence, this _____ day of _____, _____ at _____ Commonwealth of Massachusetts.

_____

The foregoing instrument was on said date subscribed at the end thereof by
_____, the above named Testator who signed, published, and declared this instrument to be his/her Last Will and Testament in the presence of us and each of us, who thereupon at his/her request, in his/her presence, and in the presence of each other, have hereunto subscribed our names as witnesses thereto. We are of sound mind and proper age to witness a will and understand this to be his/her will, and to the best of our knowledge testator is of legal age to make a will, of sound mind, and under no constraint or undue influence.

_____residing at_____

_____residing at_____

Last Will and Testament

I, _____ a resident of _____ County, Massachusetts do hereby make, publish, and declare this to be my Last Will and Testament, hereby revoking any and all Wills and Codicils heretofore made by me.

FIRST: I direct that all my just debts and funeral expenses be paid out of my estate as soon after my death as is practicable.

SECOND: I may leave a statement or list disposing of certain items of my tangible personal property. Any such statement or list in existence at the time of my death shall be determinative with respect to all items bequeathed therein.

THIRD: I give, devise, and bequeath all my estate, real, personal, and mixed, of whatever kind and wherever situated, of which I may die seized or possessed, or in which I may have any interest or over which I may have any power of appointment or testamentary disposition, as follows: _____% to my spouse, _____ and _____% to my children, _____

_____

_____,

in equal shares or to their lineal descendants per stirpes.

FOURTH: In the event that any beneficiary fails to survive me by thirty days, then this will shall take effect as if that person had predeceased me.

FIFTH: I hereby nominate, constitute, and appoint _____ as Executor of this, my Last Will and Testament. In the event that such named person is unable or unwilling to serve at any time or for any reason, then I nominate, constitute, and appoint _____ as Executor in the place and stead of the person first named herein. It is my will and I direct that my Executor shall not be required to furnish a bond for the faithful performance of his or her duties in any jurisdiction, any provision of law to the contrary notwithstanding, and I give my Executor full power to administer my estate, including the power to settle claims, pay debts, and sell, lease or exchange real and personal property without court order.

IN WITNESS WHEREOF I declare this to be my Last Will and Testament and execute it willingly as my free and voluntary act for the purposes expressed herein and I am of legal age and sound mind and make this under no constraint or undue influence, this _____ day of _____, _____ at _____ Commonwealth of Massachusetts.

_____

The foregoing instrument was on said date subscribed at the end thereof by
_____, the above named Testator who signed, published, and declared this instrument to be his/her Last Will and Testament in the presence of us and each of us, who thereupon at his/her request, in his/her presence, and in the presence of each other, have hereunto subscribed our names as witnesses thereto. We are of sound mind and proper age to witness a will and understand this to be his/her will, and to the best of our knowledge testator is of legal age to make a will, of sound mind, and under no constraint or undue influence.

_____residing at_____

_____residing at_____

Last Will and Testament

I, _____ a resident of _____ County, Massachusetts do hereby make, publish, and declare this to be my Last Will and Testament, hereby revoking any and all Wills and Codicils heretofore made by me.

FIRST: I direct that all my just debts and funeral expenses be paid out of my estate as soon after my death as is practicable.

SECOND: I may leave a statement or list disposing of certain items of my tangible personal property. Any such statement or list in existence at the time of my death shall be determinative with respect to all items bequeathed therein.

THIRD: I give, devise, and bequeath all my estate, real, personal, and mixed, of whatever kind and wherever situated, of which I may die seized or possessed, or in which I may have any interest or over which I may have any power of appointment or testamentary disposition, to my children _____

_____

_____,
plus any afterborn or adopted children in equal shares or to their lineal descendants per stirpes.

FOURTH: In the event that any beneficiary fails to survive me by thirty days, then this will shall take effect as if that person had predeceased me.

FIFTH: In the event any of my children have not attained the age of 18 years at the time of my death, I hereby nominate, constitute, and appoint _____ as guardian over the person and estate of any of my children who have not reached the age of majority at the time of my death. In the event that said guardian is unable or unwilling to serve, then I nominate, constitute, and appoint _____ as guardian. Said guardian shall serve without bond or surety.

SIXTH: I hereby nominate, constitute, and appoint _____ as Executor of this, my Last Will and Testament. In the event that such named person is unable or unwilling to serve at any time or for any reason, then I nominate, constitute, and appoint _____ as Executor in the place and stead of the person first named herein. It is my will and I direct that my Executor shall not be required to furnish a bond for the faithful performance of his or her duties in any jurisdiction, any provision of law to the contrary notwithstanding, and I give my Executor full power to administer my estate, including the power to settle claims, pay debts, and sell, lease or exchange real and personal property without court order.

IN WITNESS WHEREOF I declare this to be my Last Will and Testament and execute it willingly as my free and voluntary act for the purposes expressed herein and I am of legal age and sound mind and make this under no constraint or undue influence, this _____ day of _____, _____ at _____ Commonwealth of Massachusetts.

_____

The foregoing instrument was on said date subscribed at the end thereof by _____, the above named Testator who signed, published, and declared this instrument to be his/her Last Will and Testament in the presence of us and each of us, who thereupon at his/her request, in his/her presence, and in the presence of each other, have hereunto subscribed our names as witnesses thereto. We are of sound mind and proper age to witness a will and understand this to be his/her will, and to the best of our knowledge testator is of legal age to make a will, of sound mind, and under no constraint or undue influence.

_____residing at_____

_____residing at_____

Last Will and Testament

I, _____ a resident of _____ County, Massachusetts do hereby make, publish, and declare this to be my Last Will and Testament, hereby revoking any and all Wills and Codicils heretofore made by me.

FIRST: I direct that all my just debts and funeral expenses be paid out of my estate as soon after my death as is practicable.

SECOND: I may leave a statement or list disposing of certain items of my tangible personal property. Any such statement or list in existence at the time of my death shall be determinative with respect to all items bequeathed therein.

THIRD: I give, devise, and bequeath all my estate, real, personal, and mixed, of whatever kind and wherever situated, of which I may die seized or possessed, or in which I may have any interest or over which I may have any power of appointment or testamentary disposition, to my children _____
_____
_____,
plus any afterborn or adopted children in equal shares or to their lineal descendants per stirpes.

FOURTH: In the event that any beneficiary fails to survive me by thirty days, then this will shall take effect as if that person had predeceased me.

FIFTH: In the event any of my children have not attained the age of 18 years at the time of my death, I hereby nominate, constitute, and appoint _____ as guardian over the person of any of my children who have not reached the age of majority at the time of my death. In the event that said guardian is unable or unwilling to serve, then I nominate, constitute, and appoint _____ as guardian. Said guardian shall serve without bond or surety.

SIXTH: In the event any of my children have not attained the age of 18 years at the time of my death, I hereby nominate, constitute, and appoint _____ as guardian over the estate of any of my children who have not reached the age of majority at the time of my death. In the event that said guardian is unable or unwilling to serve, then I nominate, constitute, and appoint _____ as guardian. Said guardian shall serve without bond or surety.

SEVENTH: I hereby nominate, constitute, and appoint _____ as Executor of this, my Last Will and Testament. In the event that such named person is unable or unwilling to serve at any time or for any reason, then I nominate, constitute, and appoint _____ as Executor in the place and stead of the person first named herein. It is my will and I direct that my Executor shall not be required to furnish a bond for the faithful performance of his or her duties in any jurisdiction, any provision of law to the contrary notwithstanding, and I give my Executor full power to administer my estate, including the power to settle claims, pay debts, and sell, lease or exchange real and personal property without court order.

IN WITNESS WHEREOF I declare this to be my Last Will and Testament and execute it willingly as my free and voluntary act for the purposes expressed herein and I am of legal age and sound mind and make this under no constraint or undue influence, this _____ day of _____, _____ at _____ Commonwealth of Massachusetts.

_____

The foregoing instrument was on said date subscribed at the end thereof by _____, the above named Testator who signed, published, and declared this instrument to be his/her Last Will and Testament in the presence of us and each of us, who thereupon at his/her request, in his/her presence, and in the presence of each other, have hereunto subscribed our names as witnesses thereto. We are of sound mind and proper age to witness a will and understand this to be his/her will, and to the best of our knowledge testator is of legal age to make a will, of sound mind, and under no constraint or undue influence.

_____residing at_____

_____residing at_____

Last Will and Testament

I, _____ a resident of _____ County, Massachusetts do hereby make, publish, and declare this to be my Last Will and Testament, hereby revoking any and all Wills and Codicils heretofore made by me.

FIRST: I direct that all my just debts and funeral expenses be paid out of my estate as soon after my death as is practicable.

SECOND: I may leave a statement or list disposing of certain items of my tangible personal property. Any such statement or list in existence at the time of my death shall be determinative with respect to all items bequeathed therein.

THIRD: I give, devise, and bequeath all my estate, real, personal, and mixed, of whatever kind and wherever situated, of which I may die seized or possessed, or in which I may have any interest or over which I may have any power of appointment or testamentary disposition, to my children _____ _____ _____,

plus any afterborn or adopted children in equal shares or to their lineal descendants per stirpes.

FOURTH: In the event that any beneficiary fails to survive me by thirty days, then this will shall take effect as if that person had predeceased me.

FIFTH: In the event that any of my children have not reached the age of _____ years at the time of my death, then the share of any such child shall be held in a separate trust by _____ for such child.

The trustee shall use the income and that part of the principal of the trust as is, in the trustee's sole discretion, necessary or desirable to provide proper housing, medical care, food, clothing, entertainment and education for the trust beneficiary, considering the beneficiary's other resources. Any income that is not distributed shall be added to the principal. Additionally, the trustee shall have all powers conferred by the law of the state having jurisdiction over this trust, as well as the power to pay from the assets of the trust reasonable fees necessary to administer the trust.

The trust shall terminate when the child reaches the age specified above and the remaining assets distributed to the child, unless they have been exhausted sooner. In the event the child dies prior to the termination of the trust, then the assets shall pass to the estate of the child. The interests of the beneficiary under this trust shall not be assignable and shall be free from the claims of creditors to the full extent allowed by law.

In the event the said trustee is unable or unwilling to serve for any reason, then I nominate, constitute, and appoint _____ as alternate trustee. No bond shall be required of either trustee in any jurisdiction and this trust shall be administered without court supervision as allowed by law.

SIXTH: In the event any of my children have not attained the age of 18 years at the time of my death, I hereby nominate, constitute, and appoint _____as guardian over the person and estate of any of my children who have not reached the age of majority at the time of my death. In the event that said guardian is unable or unwilling to serve, then I nominate, constitute, and appoint _____ as guardian. Said guardian shall serve without bond or surety.

SEVENTH: I hereby nominate, constitute, and appoint _____ as Executor of this, my Last Will and Testament. In the event that such named person is unable or unwilling to serve at any time or for any reason, then I nominate, constitute, and appoint _____ as Exector in the place and stead of the person first named herein. It is my will and I direct that my Executor shall not be required to furnish a bond for the faithful performance of his or her duties in any jurisdiction, any provision of law to the contrary notwithstanding, and I give my Executor full power to administer my estate, including the power to settle claims, pay debts, and sell, lease or exchange real and personal property without court order.

IN WITNESS WHEREOF I declare this to be my Last Will and Testament and execute it willingly as my free and voluntary act for the purposes expressed herein and I am of legal age and sound mind and make this under no constraint or undue influence, this _____ day of _____, _____ at _____ Commonwealth of Massachusetts.

_____

The foregoing instrument was on said date subscribed at the end thereof by _____, the above named Testator who signed, published, and declared this instrument to be his/her Last Will and Testament in the presence of us and each of us, who thereupon at his/her request, in his/her presence, and in the presence of each other, have hereunto subscribed our names as witnesses thereto. We are of sound mind and proper age to witness a will and understand this to be his/her will, and to the best of our knowledge testator is of legal age to make a will, of sound mind, and under no constraint or undue influence.

_____residing at_____

_____residing at_____

Last Will and Testament

I, _____ a resident of _____ County, Massachusetts do hereby make, publish, and declare this to be my Last Will and Testament, hereby revoking any and all Wills and Codicils heretofore made by me.

FIRST: I direct that all my just debts and funeral expenses be paid out of my estate as soon after my death as is practicable.

SECOND: I may leave a statement or list disposing of certain items of my tangible personal property. Any such statement or list in existence at the time of my death shall be determinative with respect to all items bequeathed therein.

THIRD: I give, devise, and bequeath all my estate, real, personal, and mixed, of whatever kind and wherever situated, of which I may die seized or possessed, or in which I may have any interest or over which I may have any power of appointment or testamentary disposition, to my children _____

_____

_____,

in equal shares, or their lineal descendants per stirpes.

FOURTH: In the event that any beneficiary fails to survive me by thirty days, then this will shall take effect as if that person had predeceased me.

FIFTH: I hereby nominate, constitute, and appoint _____ as Executor of this, my Last Will and Testament. In the event that such named person is unable or unwilling to serve at any time or for any reason, then I nominate, constitute, and appoint _____ as Executor in the place and stead of the person first named herein. It is my will and I direct that my Executor shall not be required to furnish a bond for the faithful performance of his or her duties in any jurisdiction, any provision of law to the contrary notwithstanding, and I give my Executor full power to administer my estate, including the power to settle claims, pay debts, and sell, lease or exchange real and personal property without court order.

IN WITNESS WHEREOF I declare this to be my Last Will and Testament and execute it willingly as my free and voluntary act for the purposes expressed herein and I am of legal age and sound mind and make this under no constraint or undue influence, this _____ day of _____, _____ at _____ Commonwealth of Massachusetts.

_____

The foregoing instrument was on said date subscribed at the end thereof by
_____, the above named Testator who signed, published, and declared this instrument to be his/her Last Will and Testament in the presence of us and each of us, who thereupon at his/her request, in his/her presence, and in the presence of each other, have hereunto subscribed our names as witnesses thereto. We are of sound mind and proper age to witness a will and understand this to be his/her will, and to the best of our knowledge testator is of legal age to make a will, of sound mind, and under no constraint or undue influence.

_____residing at_____

_____residing at_____

Last Will and Testament

I, _____ a resident of _____ County, Massachusetts do hereby make, publish, and declare this to be my Last Will and Testament, hereby revoking any and all Wills and Codicils heretofore made by me.

FIRST: I direct that all my just debts and funeral expenses be paid out of my estate as soon after my death as is practicable.

SECOND: I may leave a statement or list disposing of certain items of my tangible personal property. Any such statement or list in existence at the time of my death shall be determinative with respect to all items bequeathed therein.

THIRD: I give, devise, and bequeath all my estate, real, personal, and mixed, of whatever kind and wherever situated, of which I may die seized or possessed, or in which I may have any interest or over which I may have any power of appointment or testamentary disposition, to my children _____

_____

_____,

in equal shares, or their lineal descendants per capita.

FOURTH: In the event that any beneficiary fails to survive me by thirty days, then this will shall take effect as if that person had predeceased me.

FIFTH: I hereby nominate, constitute, and appoint _____ as Executor of this, my Last Will and Testament. In the event that such named person is unable or unwilling to serve at any time or for any reason, then I nominate, constitute, and appoint _____ as Executor in the place and stead of the person first named herein. It is my will and I direct that my Executor shall not be required to furnish a bond for the faithful performance of his or her duties in any jurisdiction, any provision of law to the contrary notwithstanding, and I give my Executor full power to administer my estate, including the power to settle claims, pay debts, and sell, lease or exchange real and personal property without court order.

IN WITNESS WHEREOF I declare this to be my Last Will and Testament and execute it willingly as my free and voluntary act for the purposes expressed herein and I am of legal age and sound mind and make this under no constraint or undue influence, this _____ day of _____, _____ at _____ Commonwealth of Massachusetts.

_____

The foregoing instrument was on said date subscribed at the end thereof by
_____, the above named Testator who signed, published, and declared this instrument to be his/her Last Will and Testament in the presence of us and each of us, who thereupon at his/her request, in his/her presence, and in the presence of each other, have hereunto subscribed our names as witnesses thereto. We are of sound mind and proper age to witness a will and understand this to be his/her will, and to the best of our knowledge testator is of legal age to make a will, of sound mind, and under no constraint or undue influence.

_____residing at_____

_____residing at_____

Last Will and Testament

I, _____ a resident of _____
County, Massachusetts do hereby make, publish, and declare this to be my Last Will and Testament,
hereby revoking any and all Wills and Codicils heretofore made by me.

FIRST: I direct that all my just debts and funeral expenses be paid out of my estate as soon
after my death as is practicable.

SECOND: I may leave a statement or list disposing of certain items of my tangible personal
property. Any such statement or list in existence at the time of my death shall be determinative with
respect to all items bequeathed therein.

THIRD: I give, devise, and bequeath all my estate, real, personal, and mixed, of whatever
kind and wherever situated, of which I may die seized or possessed, or in which I may have any
interest or over which I may have any power of appointment or testamentary disposition, to the
following: _____
_____
_____
_____, or to the survivor of them.

FOURTH: In the event that any beneficiary fails to survive me by thirty days, then this will
shall take effect as if that person had predeceased me.

FIFTH: I hereby nominate, constitute, and appoint _____ as
Executor of this, my Last Will and Testament. In the event that such named person is unable or
unwilling to serve at any time or for any reason, then I nominate, constitute, and appoint
_____ as Executor in the place and stead of the person first named
herein. It is my will and I direct that my Executor shall not be required to furnish a bond for the
faithful performance of his or her duties in any jurisdiction, any provision of law to the contrary
notwithstanding, and I give my Executor full power to administer my estate, including the power to
settle claims, pay debts, and sell, lease or exchange real and personal property without court order.

IN WITNESS WHEREOF I declare this to be my Last Will and Testament and execute it
willingly as my free and voluntary act for the purposes expressed herein and I am of legal age and
sound mind and make this under no constraint or undue influence, this _____ day of
_____, _____ at _____ Commonwealth of Massachusetts.

_____

The foregoing instrument was on said date subscribed at the end thereof by
_____, the above named Testator who signed, published, and declared this instrument to be his/her Last Will and Testament in the presence of us and each of us, who thereupon at his/her request, in his/her presence, and in the presence of each other, have hereunto subscribed our names as witnesses thereto. We are of sound mind and proper age to witness a will and understand this to be his/her will, and to the best of our knowledge testator is of legal age to make a will, of sound mind, and under no constraint or undue influence.

_____residing at_____

_____residing at_____

Last Will and Testament

I, _____ a resident of _____ County, Massachusetts do hereby make, publish, and declare this to be my Last Will and Testament, hereby revoking any and all Wills and Codicils heretofore made by me.

FIRST: I direct that all my just debts and funeral expenses be paid out of my estate as soon after my death as is practicable.

SECOND: I may leave a statement or list disposing of certain items of my tangible personal property. Any such statement or list in existence at the time of my death shall be determinative with respect to all items bequeathed therein.

THIRD: I give, devise, and bequeath all my estate, real, personal, and mixed, of whatever kind and wherever situated, of which I may die seized or possessed, or in which I may have any interest or over which I may have any power of appointment or testamentary disposition, to the following _____ _____ _____ _____, in equal shares, or their lineal descendants per stirpes.

FOURTH: In the event that any beneficiary fails to survive me by thirty days, then this will shall take effect as if that person had predeceased me.

FIFTH: I hereby nominate, constitute, and appoint _____ as Executor of this, my Last Will and Testament. In the event that such named person is unable or unwilling to serve at any time or for any reason, then I nominate, constitute, and appoint _____ as Executor in the place and stead of the person first named herein. It is my will and I direct that my Executor shall not be required to furnish a bond for the faithful performance of his or her duties in any jurisdiction, any provision of law to the contrary notwithstanding, and I give my Executor full power to administer my estate, including the power to settle claims, pay debts, and sell, lease or exchange real and personal property without court order.

IN WITNESS WHEREOF I declare this to be my Last Will and Testament and execute it willingly as my free and voluntary act for the purposes expressed herein and I am of legal age and sound mind and make this under no constraint or undue influence, this _____ day of _____, _____ at _____ Commonwealth of Massachusetts.

_____

The foregoing instrument was on said date subscribed at the end thereof by
_____, the above named Testator who signed, published, and declared this instrument to be his/her Last Will and Testament in the presence of us and each of us, who thereupon at his/her request, in his/her presence, and in the presence of each other, have hereunto subscribed our names as witnesses thereto. We are of sound mind and proper age to witness a will and understand this to be his/her will, and to the best of our knowledge testator is of legal age to make a will, of sound mind, and under no constraint or undue influence.

_____residing at_____

_____residing at_____

Self-Proved Will Affidavit
(attach to Will)

COMMONWEALTH OF MASSACHUSETTS

COUNTY OF _____

    I, the undersigned, an officer authorized to administer oaths, certify that _____, the testator and _____, and _____, the witnesses, whose names are signed to the attached or foregoing instrument and whose signatures appear below, having appeared before me and having been first been duly sworn, each then declared to me that: 1) the attached or foregoing instrument is the last will of the testator; 2) the testator willingly and voluntarily declared, signed, and executed the will in the presence of the witnesses; 3) the witnesses signed the will upon the request of the testator, in the presence and hearing of the testator and in the presence of each other; 4) to the best knowledge of each witness, the testator was, at the time of signing, of the age of majority (or otherwise legally competent to make a will), of sound mind and memory, and under no constraint or undue influence; and 5) each witness was and is competent and of proper age to witness a will.

_____ (Testator)

_____ (Witness)

_____ (Witness)

Subscribed and sworn to before me by _____, the testator, who is personally known to me or who has produced _____ as identification, and by _____, a witness, who is personally known to me or who has produced _____ as identification, and by _____, a witness, who is personally known to me or who has produced _____ as identification, this _____ day of_____, _____.

_____

Notary or other officer

Codicil to the Will of

_____

I, _____, a resident of _____ County, Massachusetts declare this to be the first codicil to my Last Will and Testament dated _____, _____.

FIRST: I hereby revoke the clause of my Will which reads as follows:
_____
_____
_____
_____.

SECOND: I hereby add the following clause to my Will: _____
_____
_____
_____
_____.

THIRD: In all other respects I hereby confirm and republish my Last Will and Testament dated _____, _____.

IN WITNESS WHEREOF, I have signed, published, and declared the foregoing instrument as and for a codicil to my Last Will and Testament, this _____ day of _____, _____.

_____

The foregoing instrument was on the _____day of _____, _____, signed at the end thereof, and at the same time published and declared by _____, as and for a codicil to his/her Last Will and Testament, dated _____, _____, in the presence of each of us, who, this attestation clause having been read to us, did at the request of the said testator/testatrix, in his/her presence and in the presence of each other signed our names as witnesses thereto.

_____residing at_____

_____residing at_____

Self-Proved Codicil Affidavit
(attach to Codicil)

COMMONWEALTH OF _____

COUNTY OF _____

    I, the undersigned, an officer authorized to administer oaths, certify that
_____, the testator and
_____ and _____,
the witnesses, whose names are signed to the attached or foregoing instrument and whose signatures appear below, having appeared before me and having first been duly sworn, each then declared to me that: 1) the attached or foregoing instrument is a codicil to the last will of the testator; 2) the testator willingly and voluntarily declared, signed, and executed the will in the presence of the witnesses; 3) the witnesses signed the will upon the request of the testator, in the presence and hearing of the testator and in the presence of each other; 4) to the best knowledge of each witness, the testator was, at the time of signing, of the age of majority (or otherwise legally competent to make a will), of sound mind and memory, and under no constraint or undue influence; and 5) each witness was and is competent and of proper age to witness a codicil to a will.

_____ (Testator)

_____ (Witness)

_____ (Witness)

Subscribed and sworn to before me by _____, the testator, who is personally known to me or who has produced _____ as identification, and by _____ a witness who is personally known to me or who has produced _____ as identification, and by _____, a witness, who is personally known to me or who has produced _____ as identification, this _____ day of_____, _____.

_____

Notary or other officer

Living Will and Health Care Proxy of

_____

ARTICLE I: LIVING WILL

KNOW ALL MEN BY THESE PRESENTS: That I, _____, of _____, Commonwealth of Massachusetts, do hereby make, publish and declare ARTICLE I of this instrument to be my Living Will. This Living Will shall have no effect upon, and shall not revoke or cancel, any other wills, codicils or testamentary dispositions heretofore made by me. This Living Will shall also have no effect on the validity of my Health Care Proxy contained in Article II of this Instrument.

A. If my death cannot be avoided, and if I have lost the ability to interact with others and have no reasonable chance of regaining this ability, or if my suffering is intense and irreversible, I wish to have the following expressions of my desire respected and acted upon by the individuals mentioned hereinbelow:

1. I do not want to have my life prolonged.

2. I would not wish to have life support from mechanical devices or other life prolonging procedures.

Notwithstanding the foregoing, I would want to have care that gives comfort and support and that facilitates my interaction with others to the extent that is possible and which brings peace.

B. I do not fear death itself as much as the indignities of deterioration, dependence and hopeless pain. I therefore ask that medication be mercifully administered to me to alleviate suffering, even though so doing may hasten the moment of death.

ARTICLE II: HEALTH CARE PROXY

KNOW ALL MEN BY THESE PRESENTS: That I, _____ (hereinafter also the "Principal"), a legal resident of _____, Commonwealth of Massachusetts, do hereby make, publish and declare ARTICLE II of this instrument to be my HEALTH CARE PROXY and by these presents in ARTICLE II do make, constitute and appoint _____ of _____, Massachusetts my true and lawful health care agent (hereinafter the "Agent") and do hereby grant said Agent authority to make health care decisions on my behalf, said authority taking effort upon a determination, pursuant to the provisions of ARTICLE II Sections (A) and (B) below, that I lack the capacity to make or to communicate such health care decisions. It is my intention herein to appoint a health care agent and to create a valid and binding HEALTH CARE PROXY pursuant to Massachusetts General Laws ch. 201D and to comply with the provisions thereunder.

A. The determination that I lack the capacity to make or to communicate health care decisions shall be made in writing by the attending physician according to accepted standards of medical judgment and shall contain said attending physician's opinion regarding the cause and nature of my incapacity as well as the extent and probable duration of such incapacity.

B. If the attending physician determines that I have the capacity to make or to communicate health care decisions: 1) the authority of the Agent shall cease; and 2) my consent for treatment shall be required.

C. The Agent shall have the authority, pursuant to the provisions of this HEALTH CARE PROXY, to make any and all health care decisions on my behalf including decisions about life sustaining treatment after an independent doctor concurs with my physician that there is no chance of my recovery. The Agent may look to my Living Will in Article I of this instrument for guidance in making such health care decisions provided that the Agent's sole interpretation of my Living Will shall be binding and conclusive on all persons.

    D. I request that health care providers comply with the Agent's health care decisions to the same extent as if I had made such decisions.

    E. No health care provider or employee thereof shall be subject to criminal or civil liability or be deemed to have engaged in unprofessional conduct, for carrying out in good faith the Agent's health care decisions pursuant to this HEALTH CARE PROXY.

    F. No person acting as Agent pursuant to this HEALTH CARE PROXY shall be subject to criminal or civil liability for making a health care decision pursuant to this HEALTH CARE PROXY.

    G. In the event that my Agent, _____, shall be unavailable or shall for any reason, including removal, death, incapacity or resignation, cease to serve or fail to qualify as Agent hereunder, then I designate my father, _____, now or formerly of _____, _____ to serve as alternate Agent with full power and authority thereunder.

    H. In the event that any one or more of the provisions contained in this instrument shall for any reason be held to be invalid, illegal, or unenforceable in any respect, such validity, illegality or unenforceability shall not affect the validity, legality, or enforceability of any of the other provisions of this instrument.

    IN WITNESS WHEREOF, I, _____, do hereto set my hand and in the presence of the Witnesses publish and declare this Instrument, typewritten on this page and 1 other preceding sheet, one side only being used, and the preceding page having been initialed by me, to be my LIVING WILL and HEALTH CARE PROXY this _____ day of _____, _____.

_____
_____, Principal

Signed, sealed, published and declared by _____, as for, and acknowledged by _____ to be his Living Will and Health Care Proxy, in the presence of the under-signed, who at his request, in his presence and in the presence of each other, have hereunto sub-scribed our names as Witnesses the day and year first written above and hereby affirm that each of us is at least eighteen (18) years of age and that the principal appeared to be at least eighteen (18) years of age, of sound mind and under no constraint or undue influence.

_____   of   _____

_____   of   _____

COMMONWEALTH OF MASSACHUSETTS
_____, SS   Date: _____

    Then personally appeared the above _____, and acknowledged the `foregoing instrument to be his free act and deed before me,

_____
_____, Notary Public
My Commission Expires:_____

UNIFORM DONOR CARD

The undersigned hereby makes this anatomical gift, if medically acceptable, to take effect on death. The words and marks below indicate my desires:

I give:

        (a) _____ any needed organs or parts;

        (b) _____ only the following organs or parts

_____

for the purpose of transplantation, therapy, medical research, or education;

        (c) _____ my body for anatomical study if needed.

Limitations or special wishes, if any:

_____

Signed by the donor and the following witnesses in the presence of each other:

_____	_____
Signature of Donor	Date of birth
_____	_____
Date signed	City & State
_____	_____
Witness	Witness
_____	_____
Address	Address

UNIFORM DONOR CARD

The undersigned hereby makes this anatomical gift, if medically acceptable, to take effect on death. The words and marks below indicate my desires:

I give:

        (a) _____ any needed organs or parts;

        (b) _____ only the following organs or parts

_____

for the purpose of transplantation, therapy, medical research, or education;

        (c) _____ my body for anatomical study if needed.

Limitations or special wishes, if any:

_____

Signed by the donor and the following witnesses in the presence of each other:

_____	_____
Signature of Donor	Date of birth
_____	_____
Date signed	City & State
_____	_____
Witness	Witness
_____	_____
Address	Address

UNIFORM DONOR CARD

The undersigned hereby makes this anatomical gift, if medically acceptable, to take effect on death. The words and marks below indicate my desires:

I give:

        (a) _____ any needed organs or parts;

        (b) _____ only the following organs or parts

_____

for the purpose of transplantation, therapy, medical research, or education;

        (c) _____ my body for anatomical study if needed.

Limitations or special wishes, if any:

_____

Signed by the donor and the following witnesses in the presence of each other:

_____	_____
Signature of Donor	Date of birth
_____	_____
Date signed	City & State
_____	_____
Witness	Witness
_____	_____
Address	Address

UNIFORM DONOR CARD

The undersigned hereby makes this anatomical gift, if medically acceptable, to take effect on death. The words and marks below indicate my desires:

I give:

        (a) _____ any needed organs or parts;

        (b) _____ only the following organs or parts

_____

for the purpose of transplantation, therapy, medical research, or education;

        (c) _____ my body for anatomical study if needed.

Limitations or special wishes, if any:

_____

Signed by the donor and the following witnesses in the presence of each other:

_____	_____
Signature of Donor	Date of birth
_____	_____
Date signed	City & State
_____	_____
Witness	Witness
_____	_____
Address	Address

One of these cards should be cut out and carried in your wallet or purse.

Glossary

administrator (*administratrix* if female). A person appointed by the court to oversee distribution of the property of someone who died (either without a will, or if the person designated in the will is unable to serve). This person is sometimes referred to as the "personal representative"

attested will. A will which includes an attestation clause and has been signed in front of witnesses.

beneficiary. A person who is entitled to receive property from a person who died (regardless of whether there is a will).

bequest. Personal property left to someone in a will.

children's trust. A trust set up to hold property given to children. Usually it provides that the children will not receive their property until they reach a higher age than the age of majority.

codicil. An amendment to a will.

decedent. A person who has died.

descendent. A child, grandchild, great-grandchild, etc.

devise. Real property left to someone in a will. A person who is entitled to a devise is called a *devisee*.

elective share. The portion of the estate which may be taken by a surviving spouse, regardless of what the will says.

executor (*executrix* if female). A person appointed in a will to oversee distribution of the property of someone who died with a will. Sometimes this person is called a "personal representative."

exempt property. Property that is exempt from distribution as a normal part of the estate.

family allowance. An amount of money set aside from the estate to support the family of the decedent for a period of time.

forced share. *See* **elective share.**

heir. A person who will inherit from a decedent who died without a will.

holographic will. A will in which all of the material provisions are entirely in the handwriting on the maker.

intestate. Without making a will. One who dies without a will is said to have *died intestate.*

intestate share. The portion of the estate a spouse is entitled to receive if there is no will.

joint tenancy. A type of property ownership by two or more persons, in which if one owner dies, that owner's interest goes to the other joint tenants (not to the deceased owner's heirs as in tenancy in common).

legacy. Real property left to someone in a will. A person who is entitled to a legacy is called a *legatee.*

living will. A document expressing the writer's desires regarding how medical care is to be handled in the event the writer is not able to express his or her wishes concerning the use of life-prolonging medical procedures.

per capita. Distribution of property with equal shares going to each person.

per stirpes. Distribution of property with equal shares going to each family line.

probate. The process of settling a decedent's estate through the probate court.

residue. The property that is left over in an estate after all specific bequests and devises.

self-proving affidavit. A form added to a will in which the will maker and witnesses state under oath that they have signed and witnessed the will.

specific bequest *or* **specific devise**. A gift in a will of a specific item of property, or a specific amount of cash.

statutory will. A will which has been prepared according to the requirements of a statute.

tenancy by the entirety. A type of property ownership by a married couple, in which the property automatically passes to one spouse upon the death of the other. This is basically the same as joint tenancy, except that it is only between a husband and wife.

tenancy in common. Ownership of property by two or more people, in which each owner's share would descend to that owner's heirs (not to the other owners as in joint tenancy).

testate. With a will. One who dies with a will is said to have *died testate*.

testator. (*testatrix* if female.) A person who makes his or her will.

INDEX

Your #1 Source for Real World Legal Information…

SPHINX® PUBLISHING
A Division of Sourcebooks, Inc.®

- Written by lawyers
- Simple English explanation of the law
- Forms and instructions included

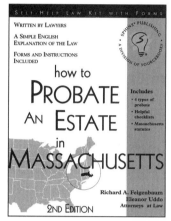

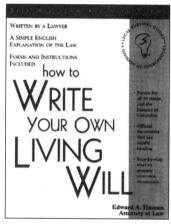

HOW TO PROBATE AN ESTATE IN MASSACHUSETTS, 2ND. ED.

A simple guide to passing on an estate in Massachusetts with minimal expense and frustration.

176 pages; $19.95;
ISBN 1-57248-109-9 November

HOW TO MAKE YOUR OWN WILL

Valid in 50 states, this book contains 14 different legal forms that will help you put your financial affairs in order. Also discusses inheritance laws.

144 pages; $12.95;
ISBN 1-57071-228-X

HOW TO WRITE YOUR OWN LIVING WILL

Step-by-step guide to writing living wills in all 50 states and the District of Columbia, complete with necessary forms.

160 pages; $9.95;
ISBN 1-57071-167-4

See the following order form for books written specifically for California, Florida, Georgia, Illinois, Massachusetts, Michigan, Minnesota, New York, North Carolina, Pennsylvania, and Texas! *Coming soon—Ohio and New Jersey!*

What our customers say about our books:

"It couldn't be more clear for the lay person." —R.D.

"I want you to know I really appreciate your book. It has saved me a lot of time and money." —L.T.

"Your real estate contracts book has saved me nearly $12,000.00 in closing costs over the past year." —A.B.

"…many of the legal questions that I have had over the years were answered clearly and concisely through your plain English interpretation of the law." —C.E.H.

"If there weren't people out there like you I'd be lost. You have the best books of this type out there." —S.B.

"…your forms and directions are easy to follow." —C.V.M.

Sphinx Publishing's Legal Survival Guides
are directly available from the Sourcebooks, Inc., or from your local bookstores.
For credit card orders call 1–800–43–BRIGHT, write P.O. Box 372, Naperville, IL 60566,
or fax 630-961-2168

SPHINX® PUBLISHING'S NATIONAL TITLES

Valid in All 50 States

LEGAL SURVIVAL IN BUSINESS

How to Form a Limited Liability Company	$19.95
How to Form Your Own Corporation (2E)	$19.95
How to Form Your Own Partnership	$19.95
How to Register Your Own Copyright (2E)	$19.95
How to Register Your Own Trademark (3E)	$19.95
Most Valuable Business Legal Forms You'll Ever Need (2E)	$19.95
Most Valuable Corporate Forms You'll Ever Need (2E)	$24.95
Software Law (with diskette)	$29.95

LEGAL SURVIVAL IN COURT

Crime Victim's Guide to Justice	$19.95
Debtors' Rights (3E)	$12.95
Defend Yourself against Criminal Charges	$19.95
Grandparents' Rights (2E)	$19.95
Help Your Lawyer Win Your Case (2E)	$12.95
Jurors' Rights (2E)	$9.95
Legal Malpractice and Other Claims against Your Lawyer (2E)	$18.95
Legal Research Made Easy (2E)	$14.95
Simple Ways to Protect Yourself from Lawsuits	$24.95
Victims' Rights	$12.95
Winning Your Personal Injury Claim	$19.95

LEGAL SURVIVAL IN REAL ESTATE

How to Buy a Condominium or Townhome	$16.95
How to Negotiate Real Estate Contracts (3E)	$16.95
How to Negotiate Real Estate Leases (3E)	$16.95
Successful Real Estate Brokerage Management	$19.95

LEGAL SURVIVAL IN PERSONAL AFFAIRS

Your Right to Child Custody, Visitation and Support	$19.95
The Nanny and Domestic Help Legal Kit	$19.95
How to File Your Own Bankruptcy (4E)	$19.95
How to File Your Own Divorce (3E)	$19.95
How to Make Your Own Will	$12.95
How to Write Your Own Living Will	$9.95
How to Write Your Own Premarital Agreement (2E)	$19.95
How to Win Your Unemployment Compensation Claim	$19.95
Living Trusts and Simple Ways to Avoid Probate (2E)	$19.95
Neighbor v. Neighbor (2E)	$12.95
The Power of Attorney Handbook (3E)	$19.95
Simple Ways to Protect Yourself from Lawsuits	$24.95
Social Security Benefits Handbook (2E)	$14.95
Unmarried Parents' Rights	$19.95
U.S.A. Immigration Guide (3E)	$19.95
Guia de Inmigracion a Estados Unidos (2E)	$19.95

Legal Survival Guides are directly available from Sourcebooks, Inc., or from your local bookstores.

For credit card orders call 1–800–43–BRIGHT, write P.O. Box 372, Naperville, IL 60566,
or fax 630-961-2168

SPHINX® PUBLISHING ORDER FORM

<table>
<tr><td>BILL TO:</td><td>SHIP TO:</td></tr>
</table>

Phone #	Terms	F.O.B.	Chicago, IL	Ship Date

Charge my: ☐ VISA   ☐ MasterCard   ☐ American Express

☐ **Money Order or Personal Check**

Credit Card Number

Expiration Date

Qty	ISBN	Title	Retail	Ext.
		SPHINX PUBLISHING NATIONAL TITLES		
_____	1-57071-166-6	Crime Victim's Guide to Justice	$19.95	_____
_____	1-57071-342-1	Debtors' Rights (3E)	$12.95	_____
_____	1-57071-162-3	Defend Yourself against Criminal Charges	$19.95	_____
_____	1-57248-082-3	Grandparents' Rights (2E)	$19.95	_____
_____	1-57248-087-4	Guia de Inmigracion a Estados Unidos (2E)	$19.95	_____
_____	1-57248-103-X	Help Your Lawyer Win Your Case (2E)	$12.95	_____
_____	1-57071-164-X	How to Buy a Condominium or Townhome	$16.95	_____
_____	1-57071-223-9	How to File Your Own Bankruptcy (4E)	$19.95	_____
_____	1-57071-224-7	How to File Your Own Divorce (3E)	$19.95	_____
_____	1-57248-083-1	How to Form a Limited Liability Company	$19.95	_____
_____	1-57248-099-8	How to Form a Nonprofit Corporation	$24.95	_____
_____	1-57071-227-1	How to Form Your Own Corporation (2E)	$19.95	_____
_____	1-57071-343-X	How to Form Your Own Partnership	$19.95	_____
_____	1-57071-228-X	How to Make Your Own Will	$12.95	_____
_____	1-57071-331-6	How to Negotiate Real Estate Contracts (3E)	$16.95	_____
_____	1-57071-332-4	How to Negotiate Real Estate Leases (3E)	$16.95	_____
_____	1-57071-225-5	How to Register Your Own Copyright (2E)	$19.95	_____
_____	1-57248-104-8	How to Register Your Own Trademark (3E)	$19.95	_____
_____	1-57071-349-9	How to Win Your Unemployment Compensation Claim	$19.95	_____
_____	1-57071-167-4	How to Write Your Own Living Will	$9.95	_____
_____	1-57071-344-8	How to Write Your Own Premarital Agreement (2E)	$19.95	_____
_____	1-57071-333-2	Jurors' Rights (2E)	$9.95	_____
_____	1-57248-032-7	Legal Malpractice and Other Claims against...	$18.95	_____
_____	1-57071-400-2	Legal Research Made Easy (2E)	$14.95	_____
_____	1-57071-336-7	Living Trusts and Simple Ways to Avoid Probate (2E)	$19.95	_____
_____	1-57071-345-6	Most Valuable Bus. Legal Forms You'll Ever Need (2E)	$19.95	_____
_____	1-57071-346-4	Most Valuable Corporate Forms You'll Ever Need (2E)	$24.95	_____
_____	1-57248-089-0	Neighbor v. Neighbor (2E)	$12.95	_____
_____	1-57071-348-0	The Power of Attorney Handbook (3E)	$19.95	_____

Qty	ISBN	Title	Retail	Ext.
_____	1-57248-020-3	Simple Ways to Protect Yourself from Lawsuits	$24.95	_____
_____	1-57071-337-5	Social Security Benefits Handbook (2E)	$14.95	_____
_____	1-57071-163-1	Software Law (w/diskette)	$29.95	_____
_____	0-913825-86-7	Successful Real Estate Brokerage Mgmt.	$19.95	_____
_____	1-57248-098-X	The Nanny and Domestic Help Legal Kit	$19.95	_____
_____	1-57071-399-5	Unmarried Parents' Rights	$19.95	_____
_____	1-57071-354-5	U.S.A. Immigration Guide (3E)	$19.95	_____
_____	0-913825-82-4	Victims' Rights	$12.95	_____
_____	1-57071-165-8	Winning Your Personal Injury Claim	$19.95	_____
_____	1-57248-097-1	Your Right to Child Custody, Visitation and Support	$19.95	_____
		CALIFORNIA TITLES		
_____	1-57071-360-X	CA Power of Attorney Handbook	$12.95	_____
_____	1-57071-355-3	How to File for Divorce in CA	$19.95	_____
_____	1-57071-356-1	How to Make a CA Will	$12.95	_____
_____	1-57071-408-8	How to Probate an Estate in CA	$19.95	_____
_____	1-57071-357-X	How to Start a Business in CA	$16.95	_____
_____	1-57071-358-8	How to Win in Small Claims Court in CA	$14.95	_____
_____	1-57071-359-6	Landlords' Rights and Duties in CA	$19.95	_____
		NEW YORK TITLES		
_____	1-57071-184-4	How to File for Divorce in NY	$19.95	_____
		FLORIDA TITLES		
_____	1-57071-363-4	Florida Power of Attorney Handbook (2E)	$12.95	_____
_____	1-57248-093-9	How to File for Divorce in FL (6E)	$21.95	_____
_____	1-57248-086-6	How to Form a Limited Liability Co. in FL	$19.95	_____
_____	1-57071-401-0	How to Form a Partnership in FL	$19.95	_____
_____	1-57071-380-4	How to Form a Corporation in FL (4E)	$19.95	_____
_____	1-57071-361-8	How to Make a FL Will (5E)	$12.95	_____
_____	1-57248-088-2	How to Modify Your FL Divorce Judgment (4E)	$22.95	_____
_____		*Form Continued on Following Page*	**SUBTOTAL**	_____

To order, call Sourcebooks at 1-800-43-BRIGHT or FAX (630)961-2168 (Bookstores, libraries, wholesalers—please call for discount)

SPHINX® PUBLISHING ORDER FORM

Qty	ISBN	Title	Retail	Ext.
		FLORIDA TITLES (CONT'D)		
	1-57071-364-2	How to Probate an Estate in FL (3E)	$24.95	
	1-57248-081-5	How to Start a Business in FL (5E)	$16.95	
	1-57071-362-6	How to Win in Small Claims Court in FL (6E)	$14.95	
	1-57071-335-9	Landlords' Rights and Duties in FL (7E)	$19.95	
	1-57071-334-0	Land Trusts in FL (5E)	$24.95	
	0-913825-73-5	Women's Legal Rights in FL	$19.95	
		GEORGIA TITLES		
	1-57071-376-6	How to File for Divorce in GA (3E)	$19.95	
	1-57248-075-0	How to Make a GA Will (3E)	$12.95	
	1-57248-076-9	How to Start a Business in Georgia (3E)	$16.95	
		ILLINOIS TITLES		
	1-57071-405-3	How to File for Divorce in IL (2E)	$19.95	
	1-57071-415-0	How to Make an IL Will (2E)	$12.95	
	1-57071-416-9	How to Start a Business in IL (2E)	$16.95	
	1-57248-078-5	Landlords' Rights & Duties in IL	$19.95	
		MASSACHUSETTS TITLES		
	1-57071-329-4	How to File for Divorce in MA (2E)	$19.95	
	1-57248-108-0	How to Make a MA Will (2E)	$12.95	
	1-57248-109-9	How to Probate an Estate in MA (2E)	$19.95	
	1-57248-106-4	How to Start a Business in MA (2E)	$16.95	
	1-57248-107-2	Landlords' Rights and Duties in MA (2E)	$19.95	
		MICHIGAN TITLES		
	1-57071-409-6	How to File for Divorce in MI (2E)	$19.95	
	1-57248-077-7	How to Make a MI Will (2E)	$12.95	
	1-57071-407-X	How to Start a Business in MI (2E)	$16.95	
		MINNESOTA TITLES		
	1-57248-039-4	How to File for Divorce in MN	$19.95	
	1-57248-040-8	How to Form a Simple Corporation in MN	$19.95	
	1-57248-037-8	How to Make a MN Will	$9.95	
	1-57248-038-6	How to Start a Business in MN	$16.95	
		NEVADA TITLES		
	1-57248-101-3	How to Form a Corporation in NV	$19.95	
		NEW YORK TITLES		
	1-57071-184-4	How to File for Divorce in NY	$19.95	

Qty	ISBN	Title	Retail	Ext.
	1-57248-105-6	How to Form a Corporation in NY	$19.95	
	1-57248-095-5	How to Make a NY Will (2E)	$12.95	
	1-57071-185-2	How to Start a Business in NY	$16.95	
	1-57071-187-9	How to Win in Small Claims Court in NY	$14.95	
	1-57071-186-0	Landlords' Rights and Duties in NY	$19.95	
	1-57071-188-7	New York Power of Attorney Handbook	$19.95	
		NORTH CAROLINA TITLES		
	1-57071-326-X	How to File for Divorce in NC (2E)	$19.95	
	1-57071-327-8	How to Make a NC Will (2E)	$12.95	
	1-57248-096-3	How to Start a Business in NC (2E)	$16.95	
	1-57248-091-2	Landlords' Rights & Duties in NC	$19.95	
		OHIO TITLES		
	1-57248-102-1	How to File for Divorce in OH	$19.95	
		PENNSYLVANIA TITLES		
	1-57071-177-1	How to File for Divorce in PA	$19.95	
	1-57248-094-7	How to Make a PA Will (2E)	$12.95	
	1-57248-112-9	How to Start a Business in PA (2E)	$16.95	
	1-57071-179-8	Landlords' Rights and Duties in PA	$19.95	
		TEXAS TITLES		
	1-57071-330-8	How to File for Divorce in TX (2E)	$19.95	
	1-57248-009-2	How to Form a Simple Corporation in TX	$19.95	
	1-57071-417-7	How to Make a TX Will (2E)	$12.95	
	1-57071-418-5	How to Probate an Estate in TX (2E)	$19.95	
	1-57071-365-0	How to Start a Business in TX (2E)	$16.95	
	1-57248-111-0	How to Win in Small Claims Court in TX (2E)	$14.95	
	1-57248-110-2	Landlords' Rights and Duties in TX (2E)	$19.95	

SUBTOTAL THIS PAGE _____

SUBTOTAL PREVIOUS PAGE _____

Illinois residents add 6.75% sales tax _____

Florida residents add 6% state sales tax plus applicable discretionary surtax _____

Shipping— $4.00 for 1st book, $1.00 each additional _____

TOTAL _____